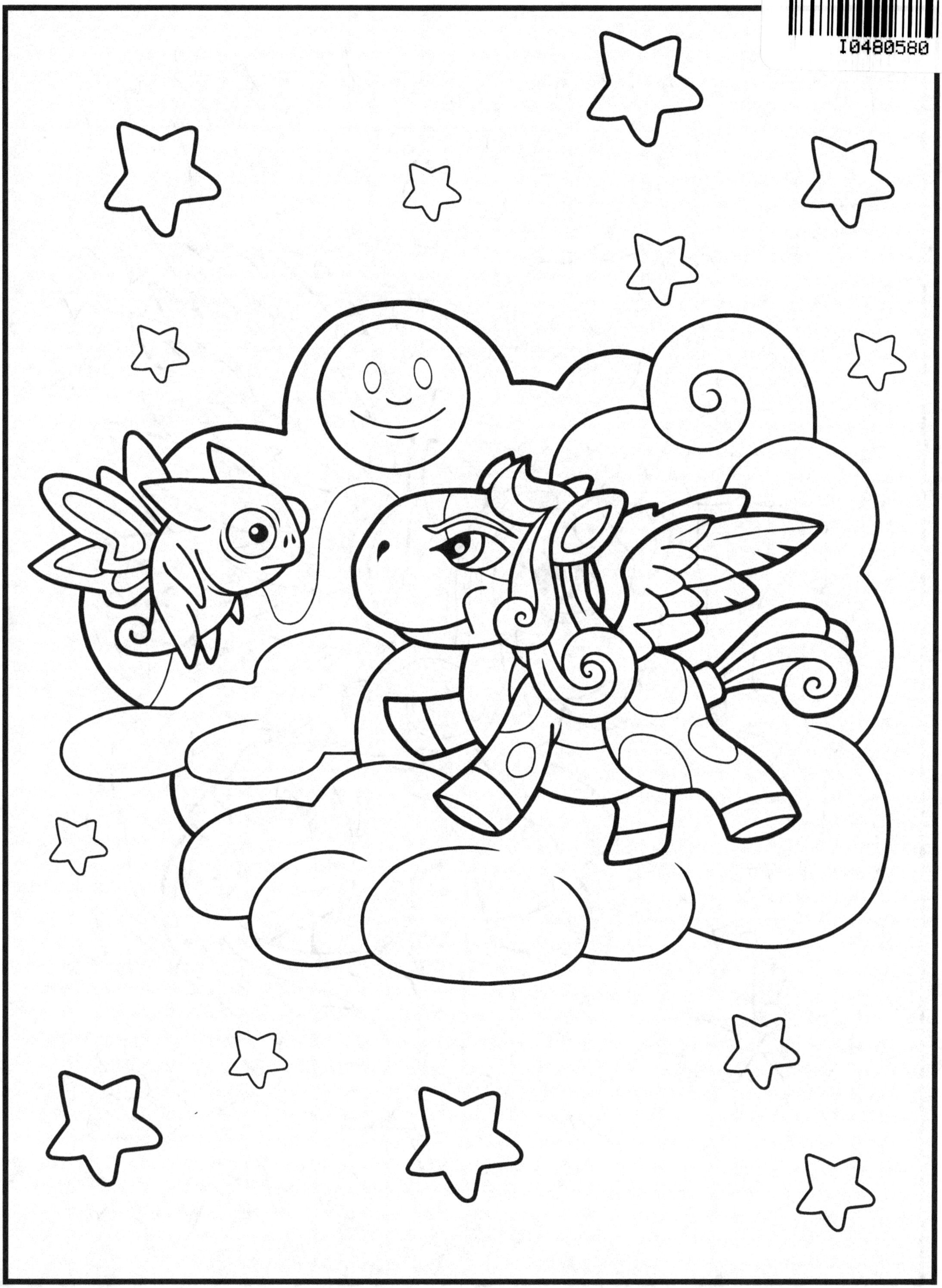

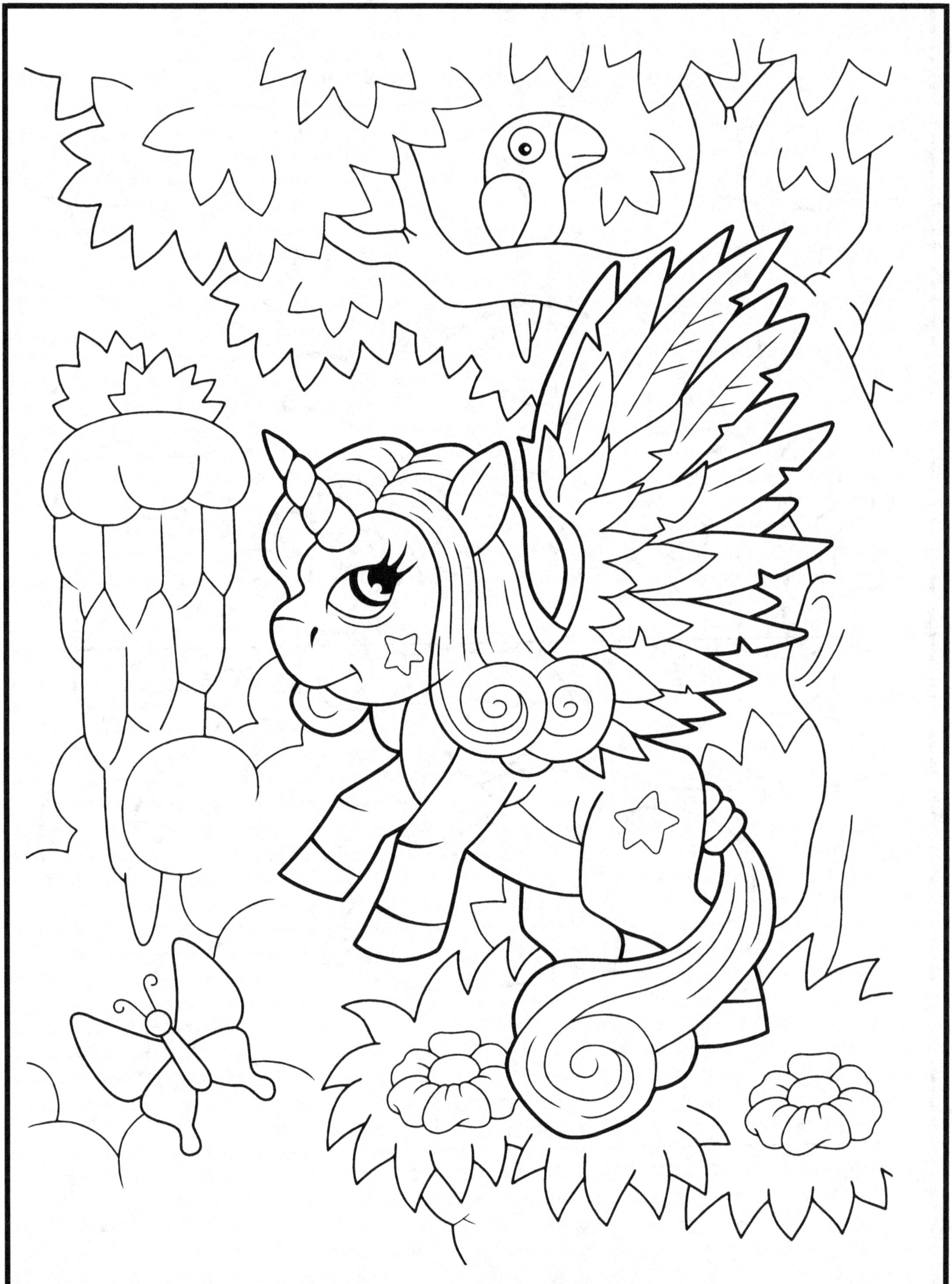

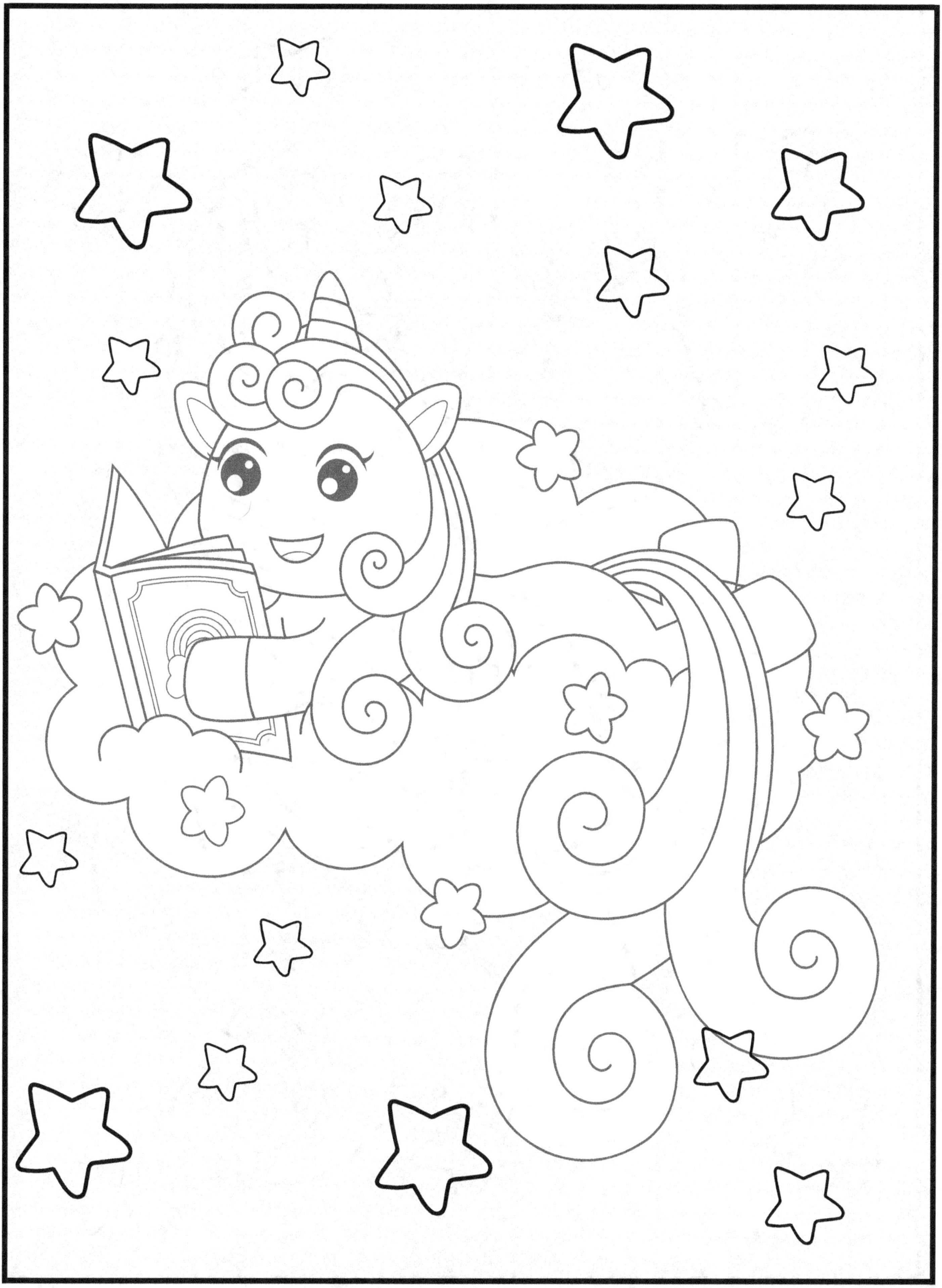

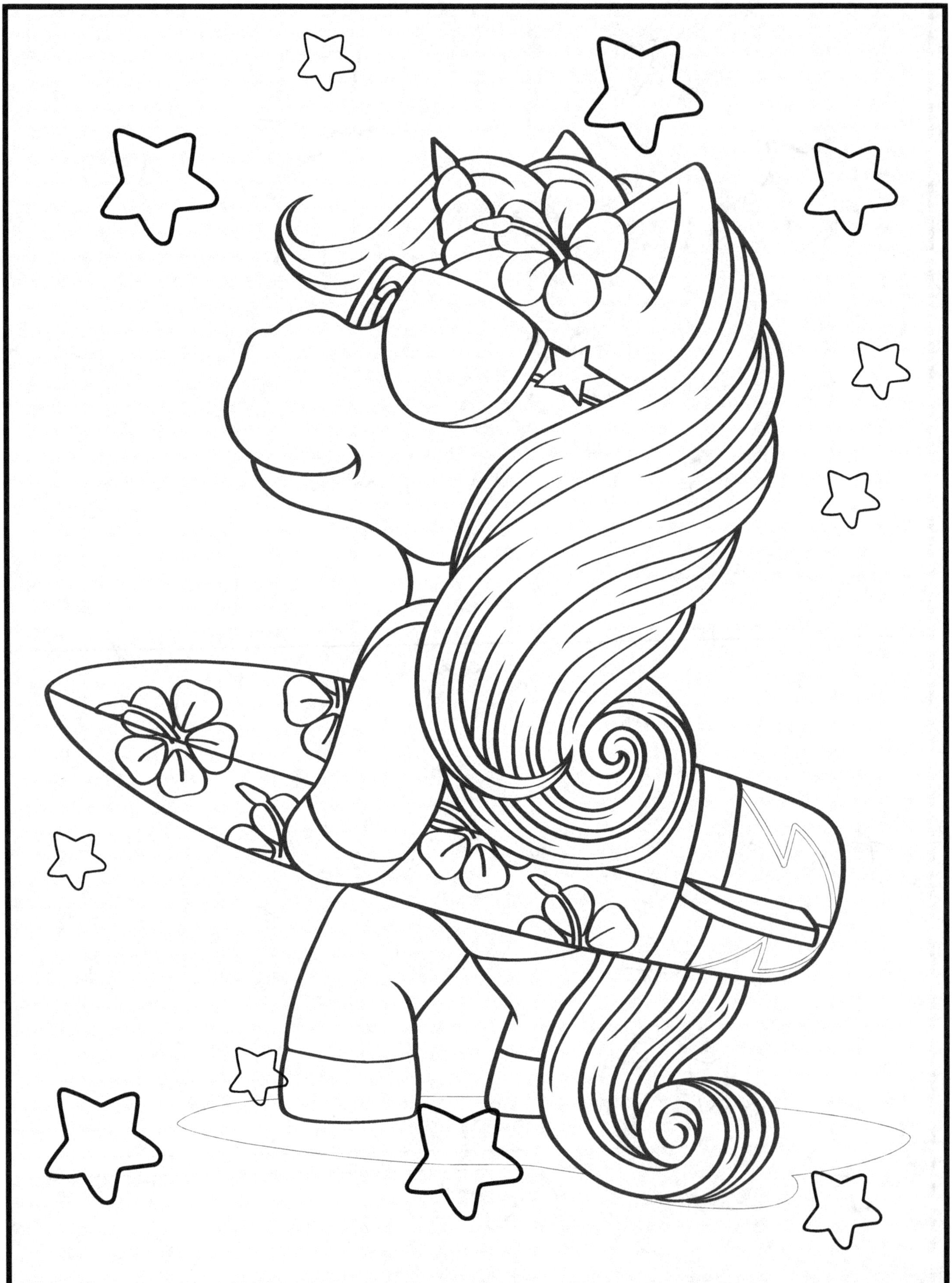

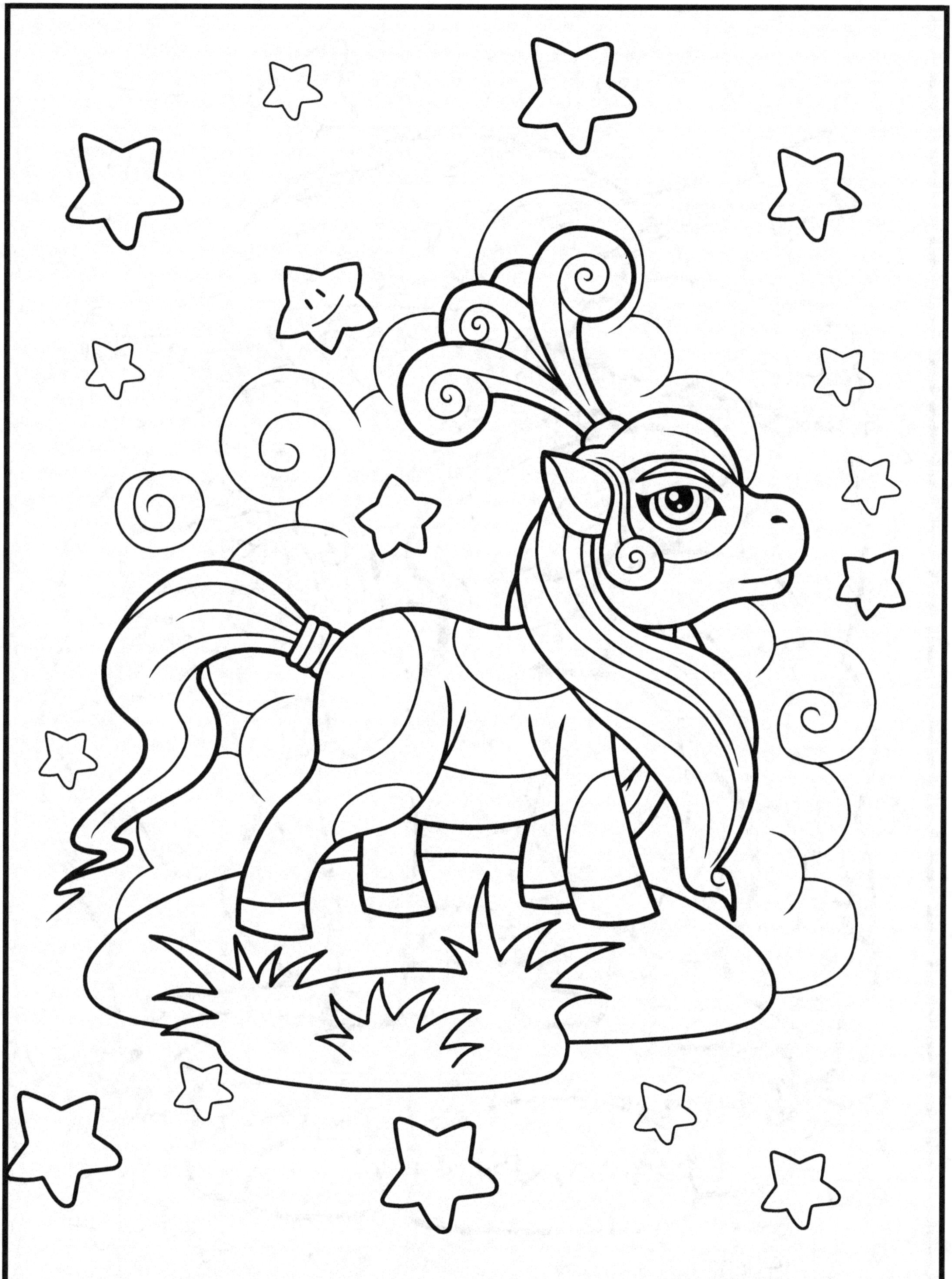

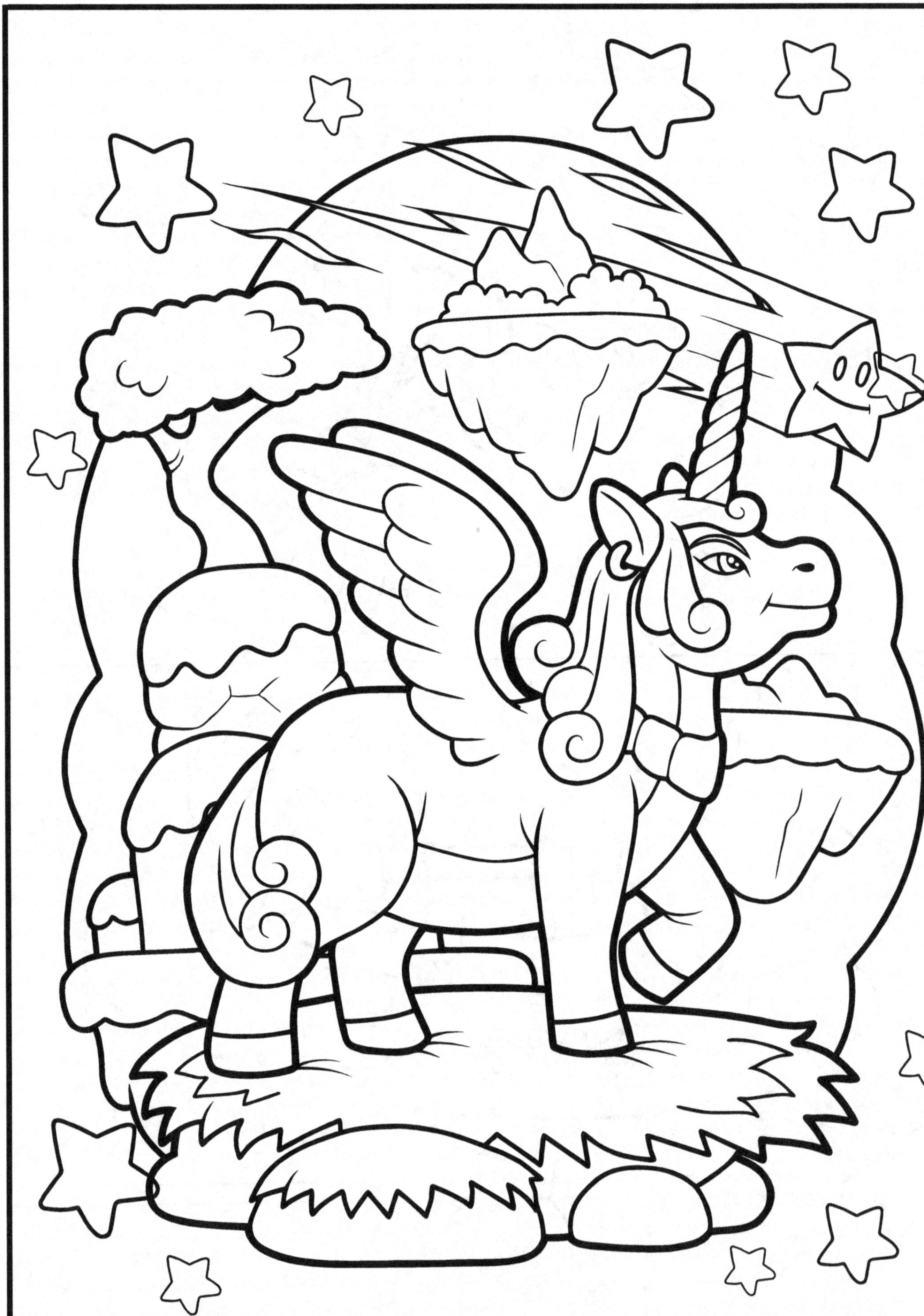

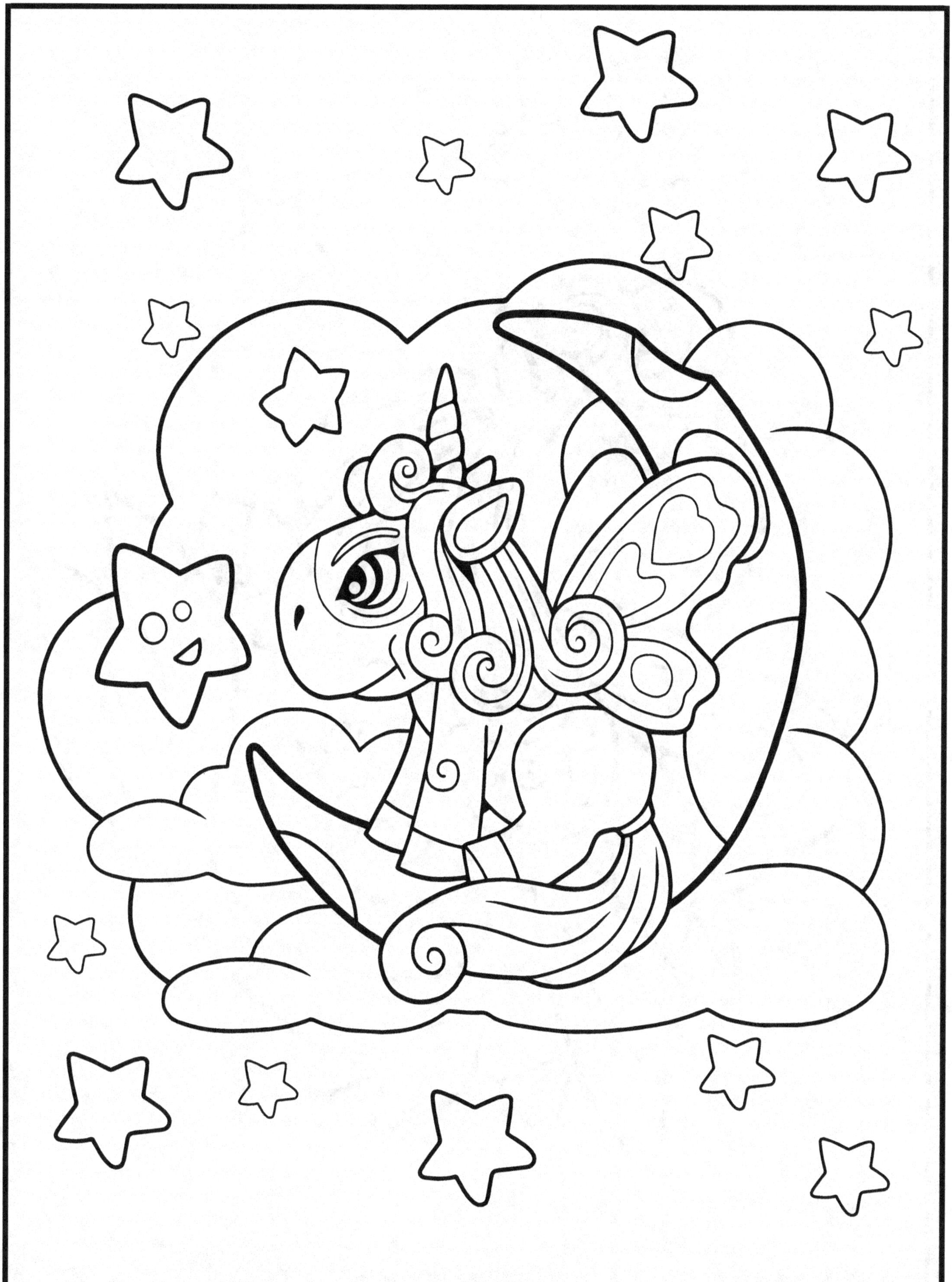

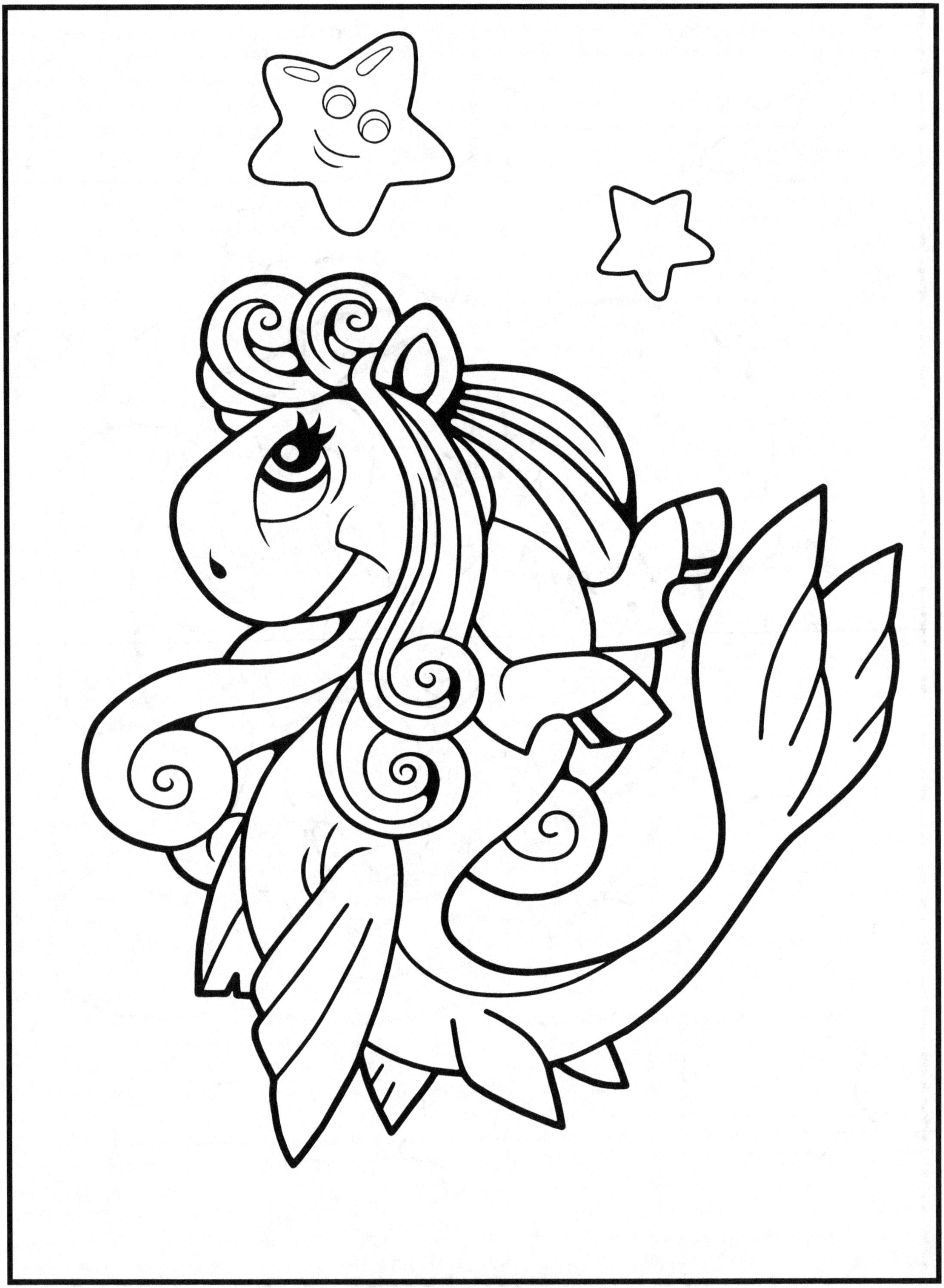

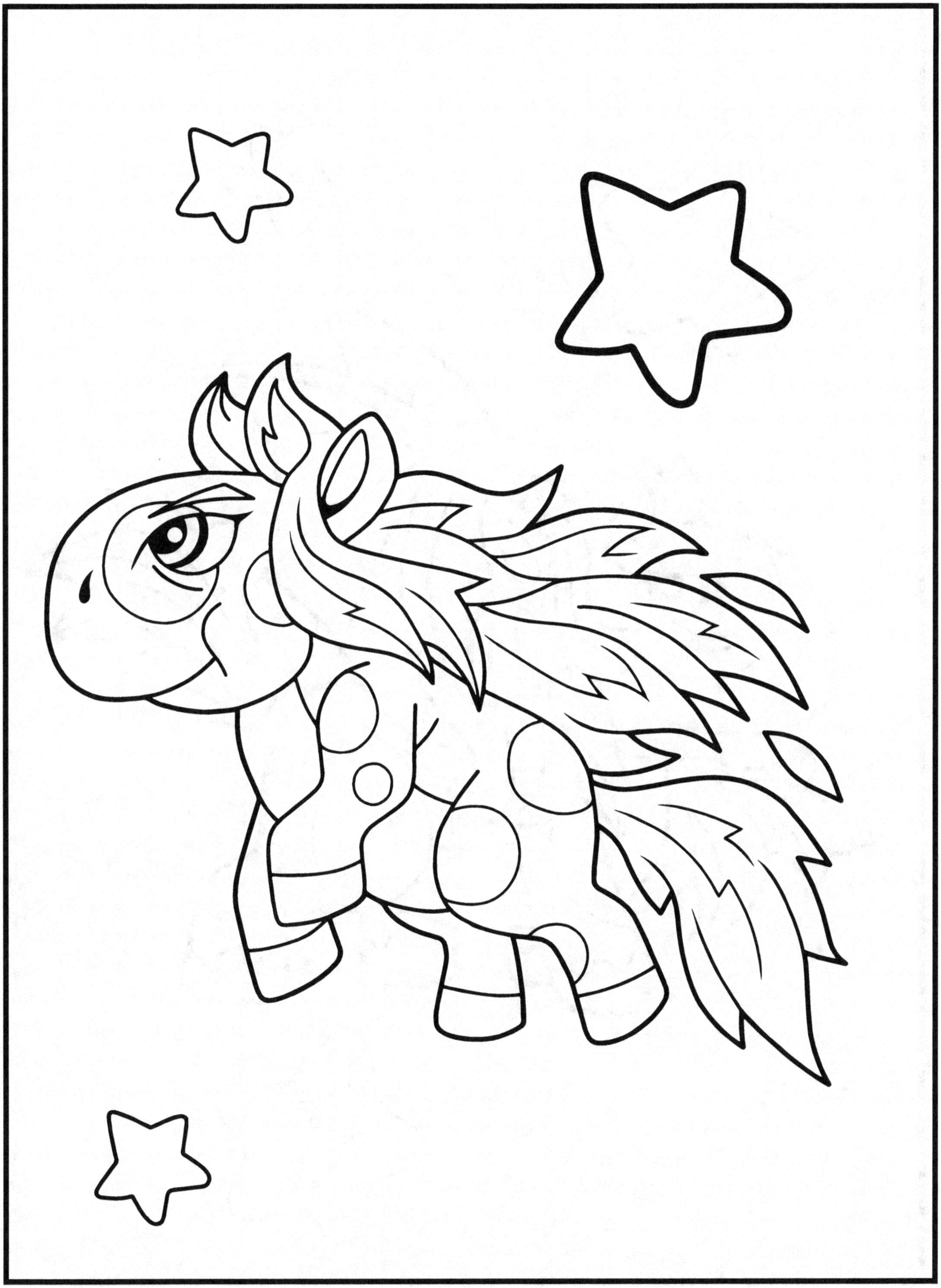

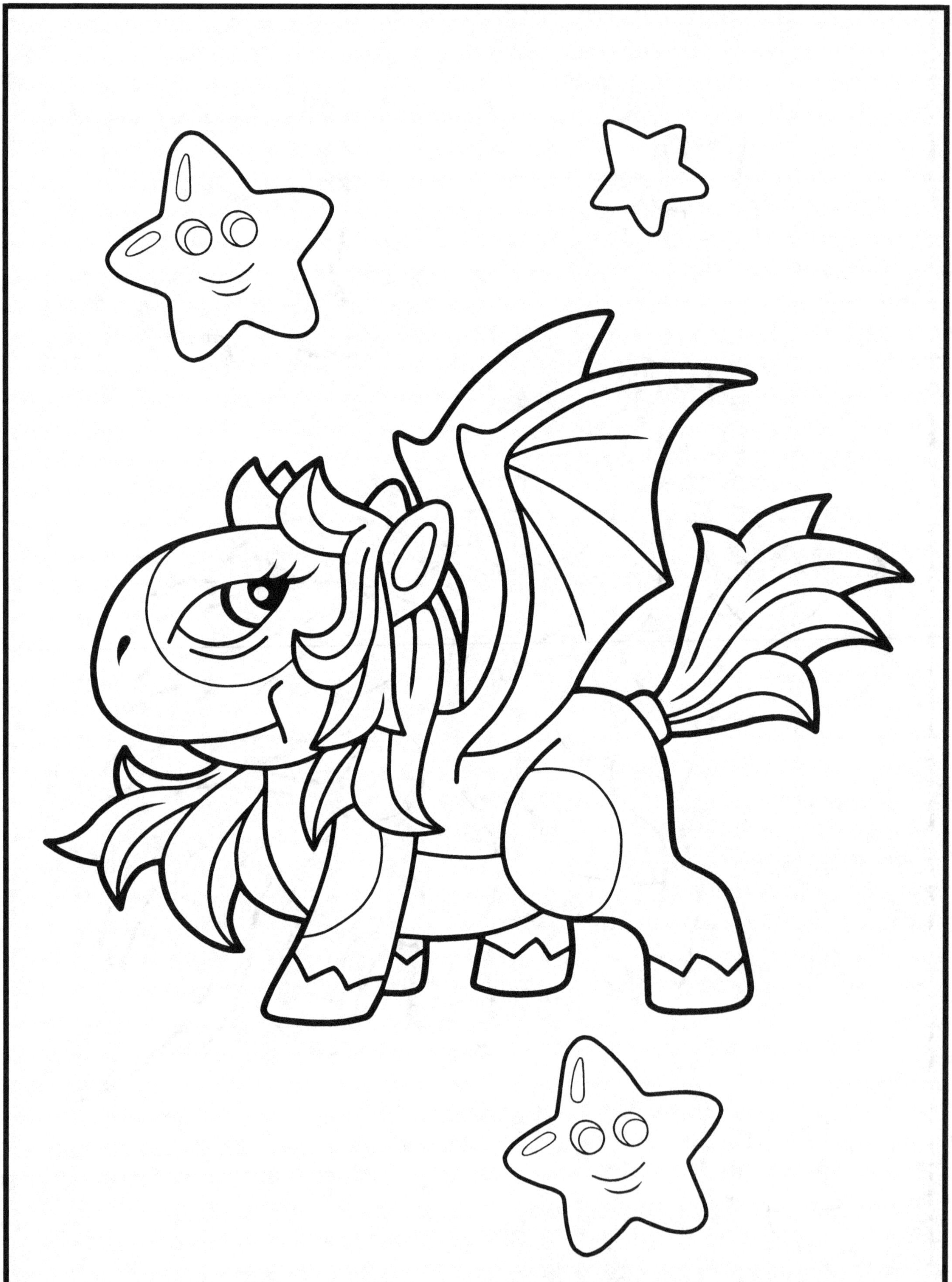

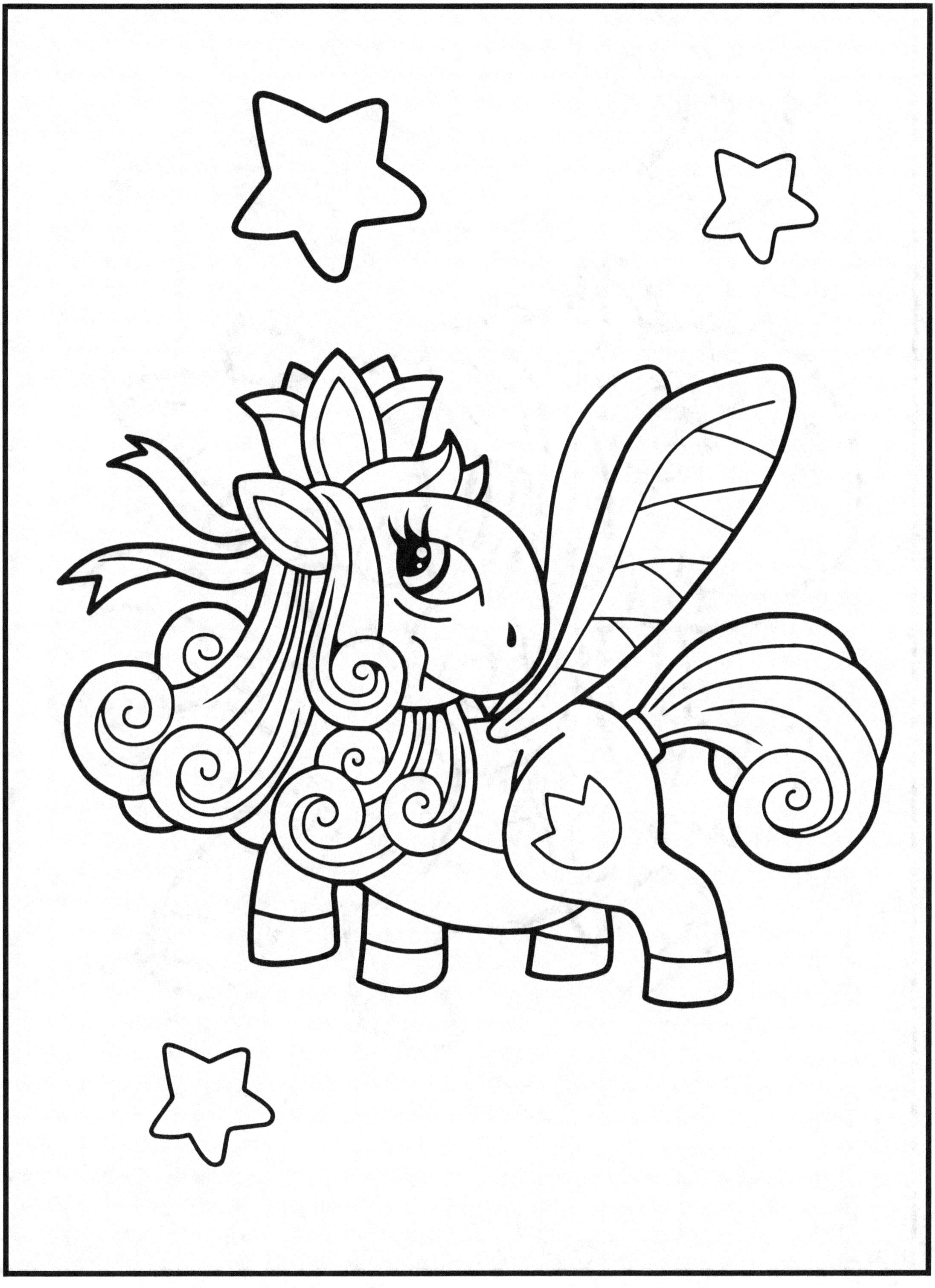

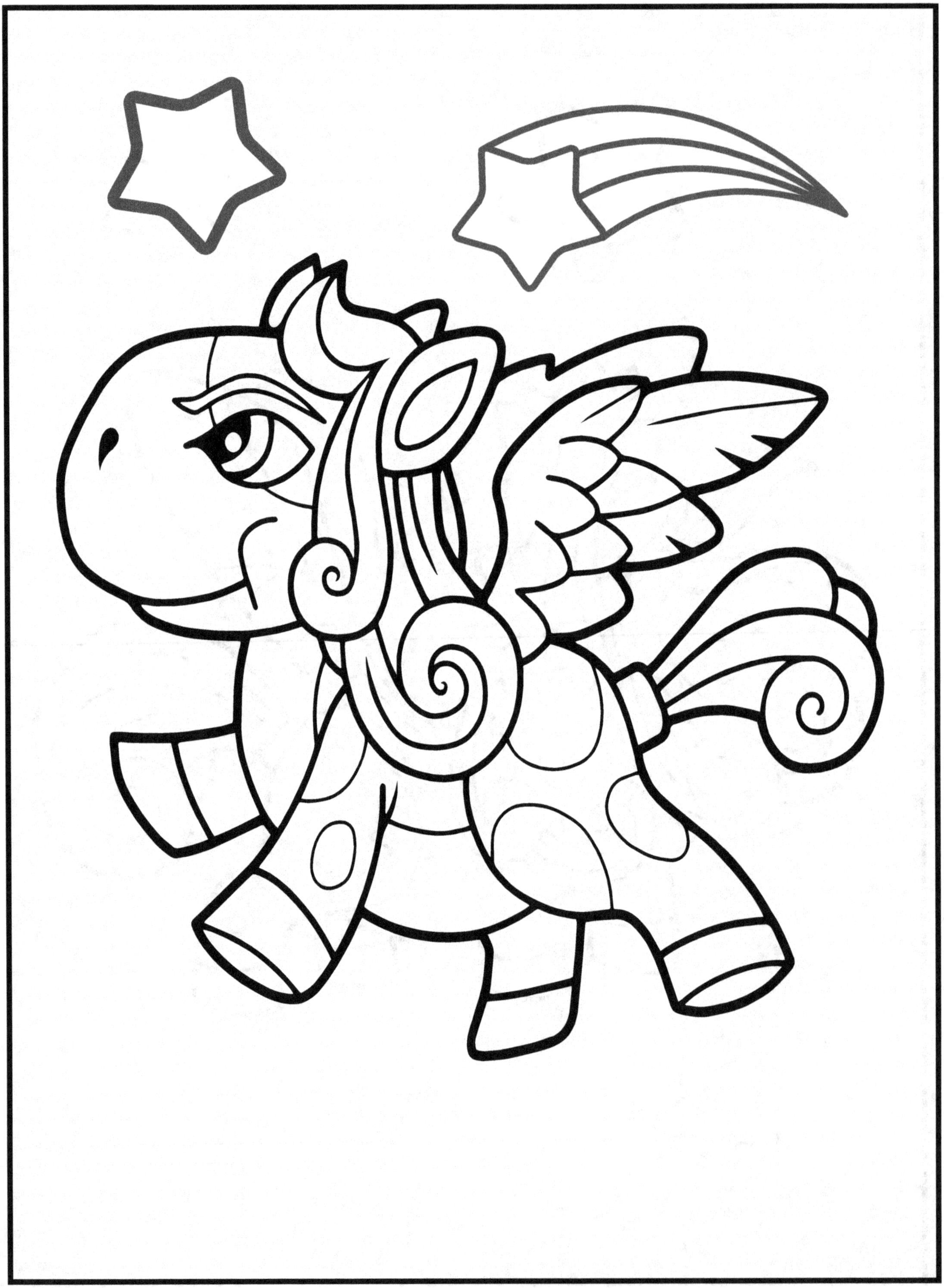

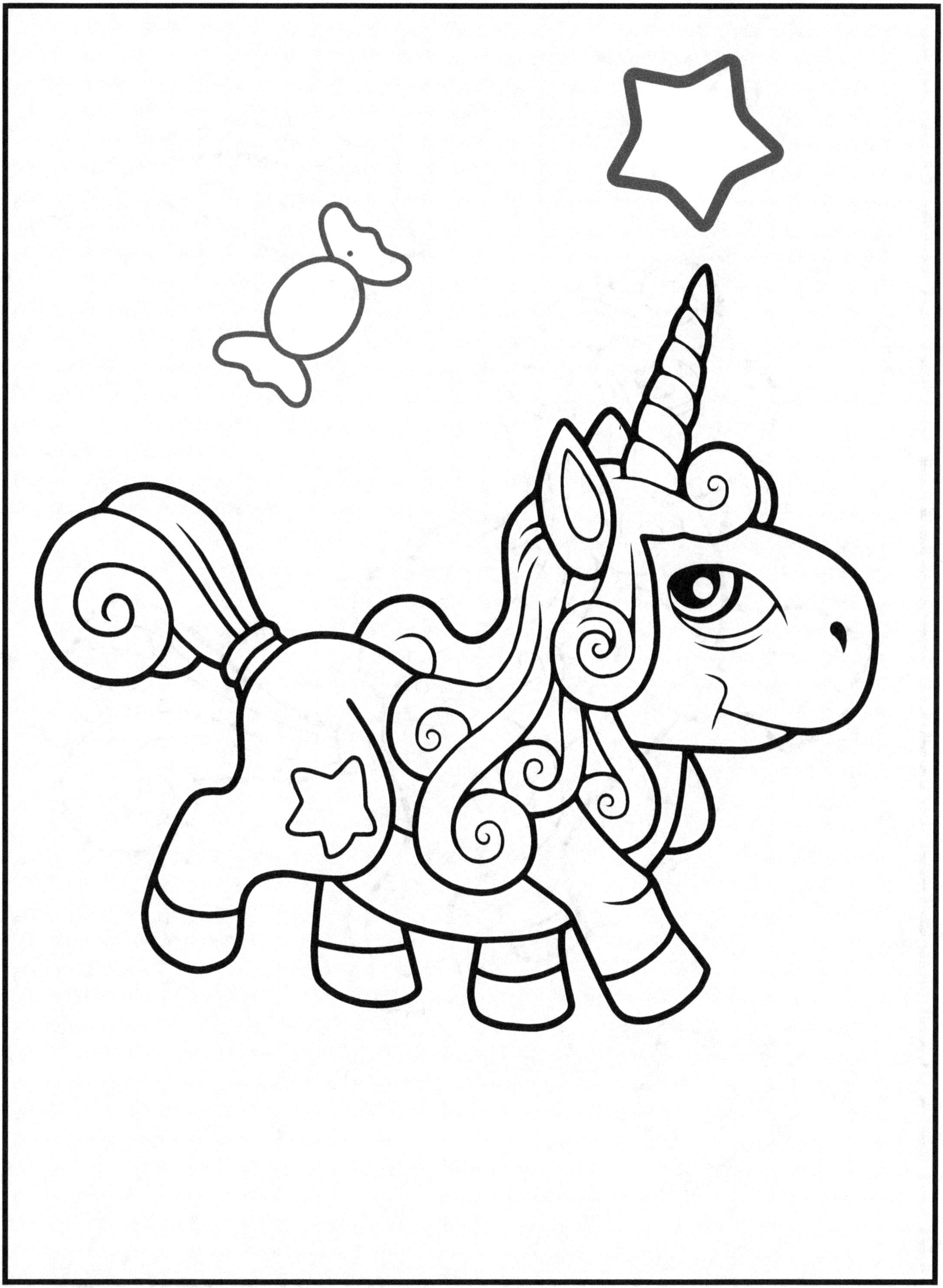

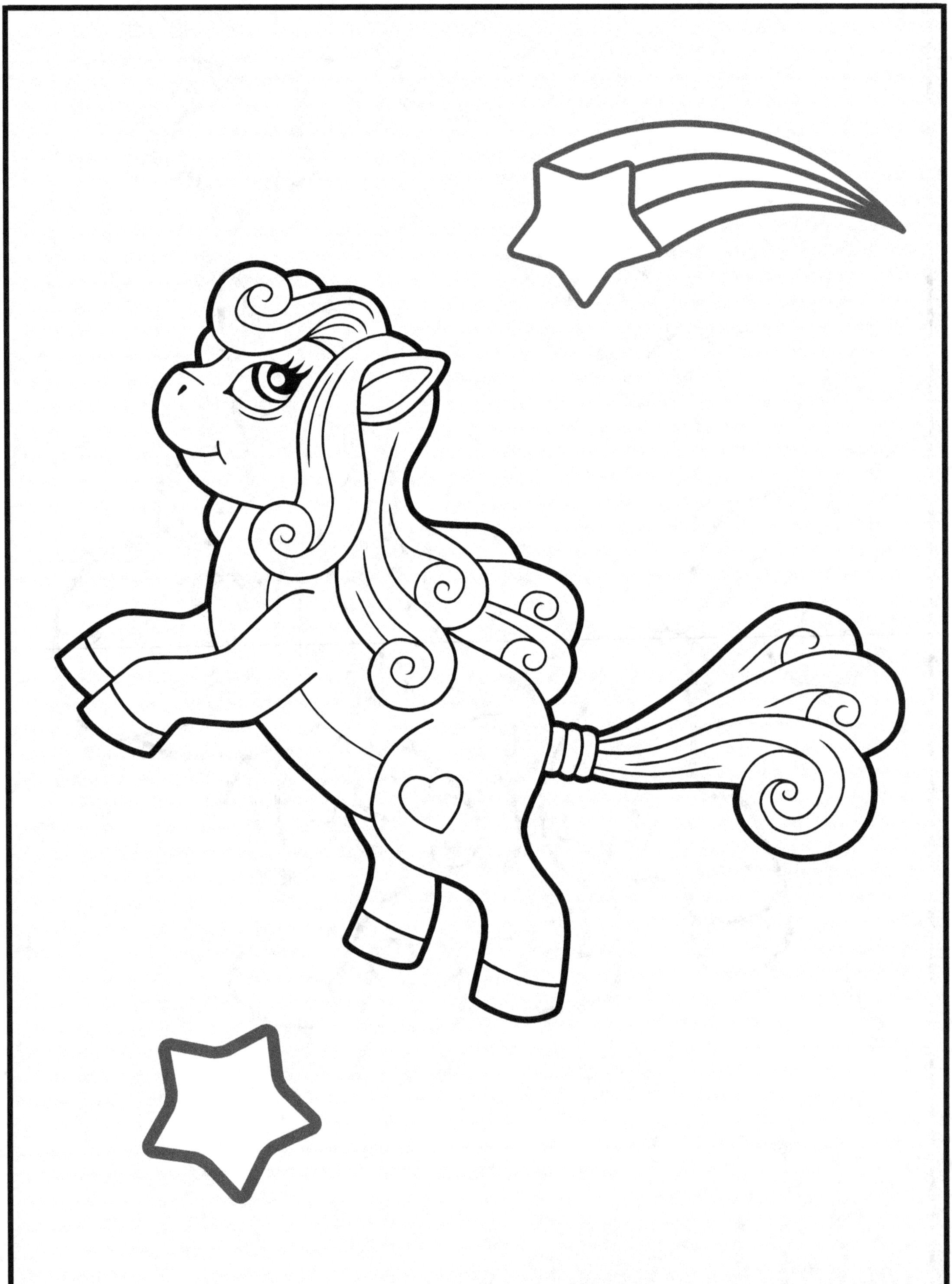

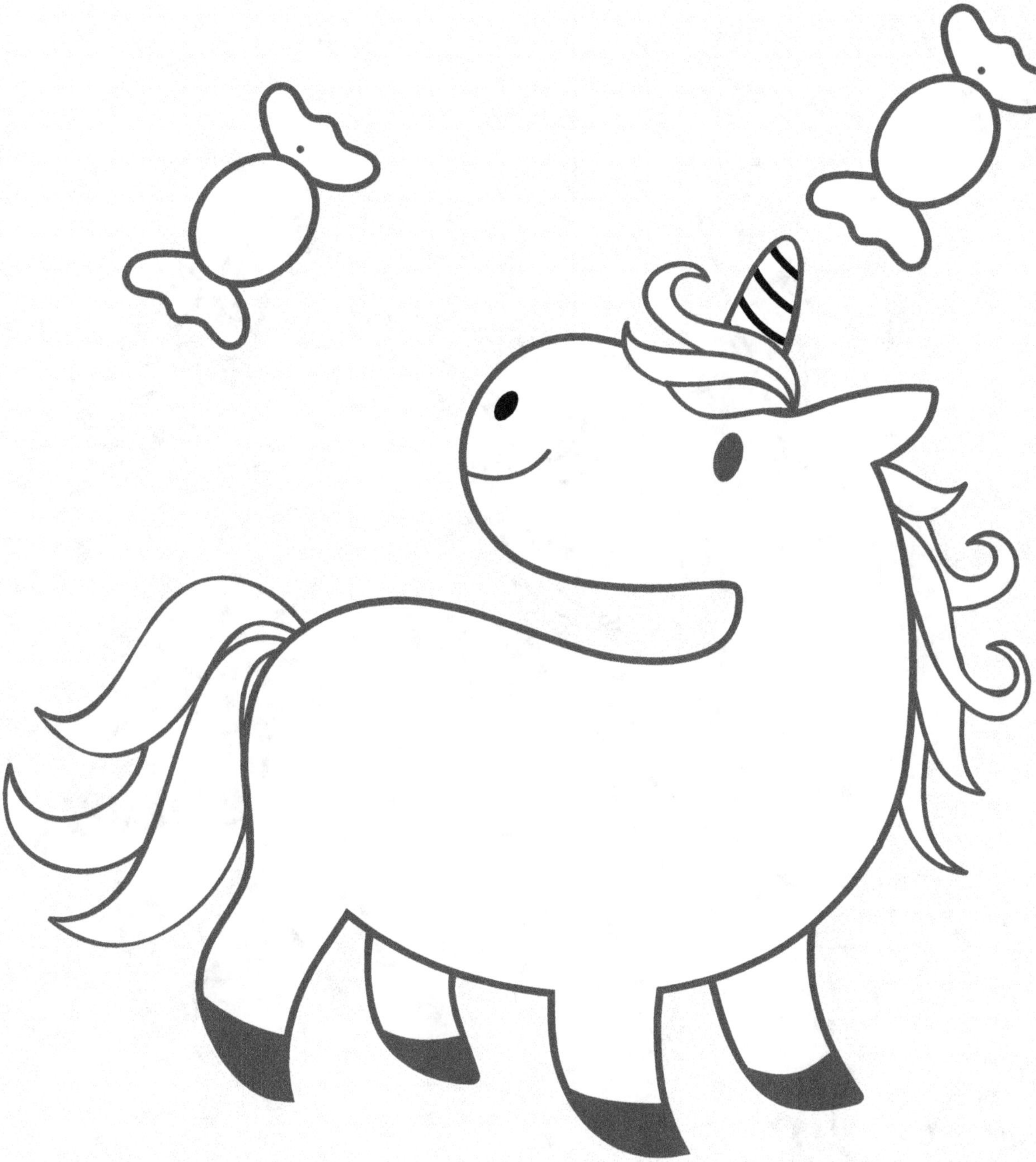

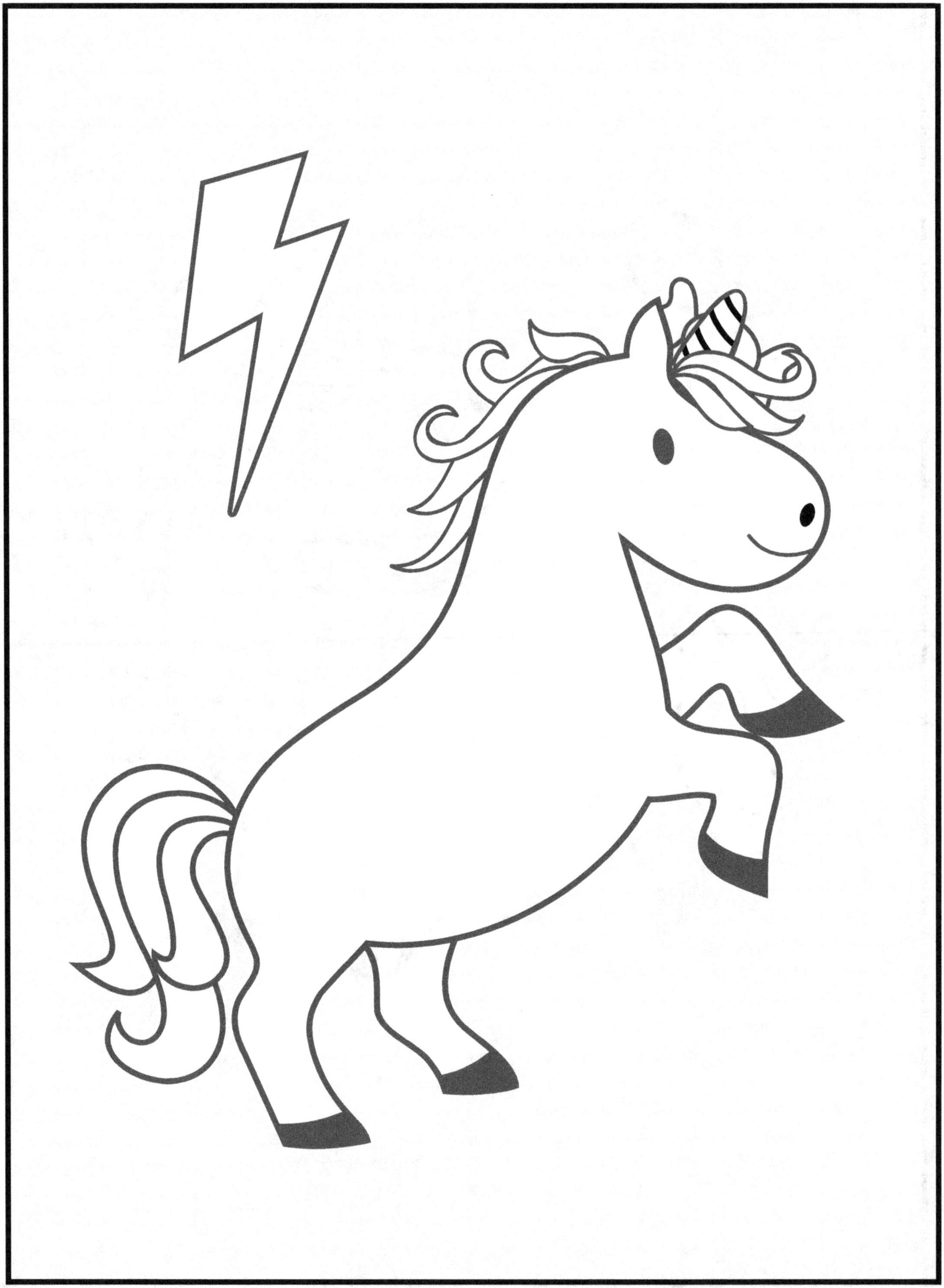

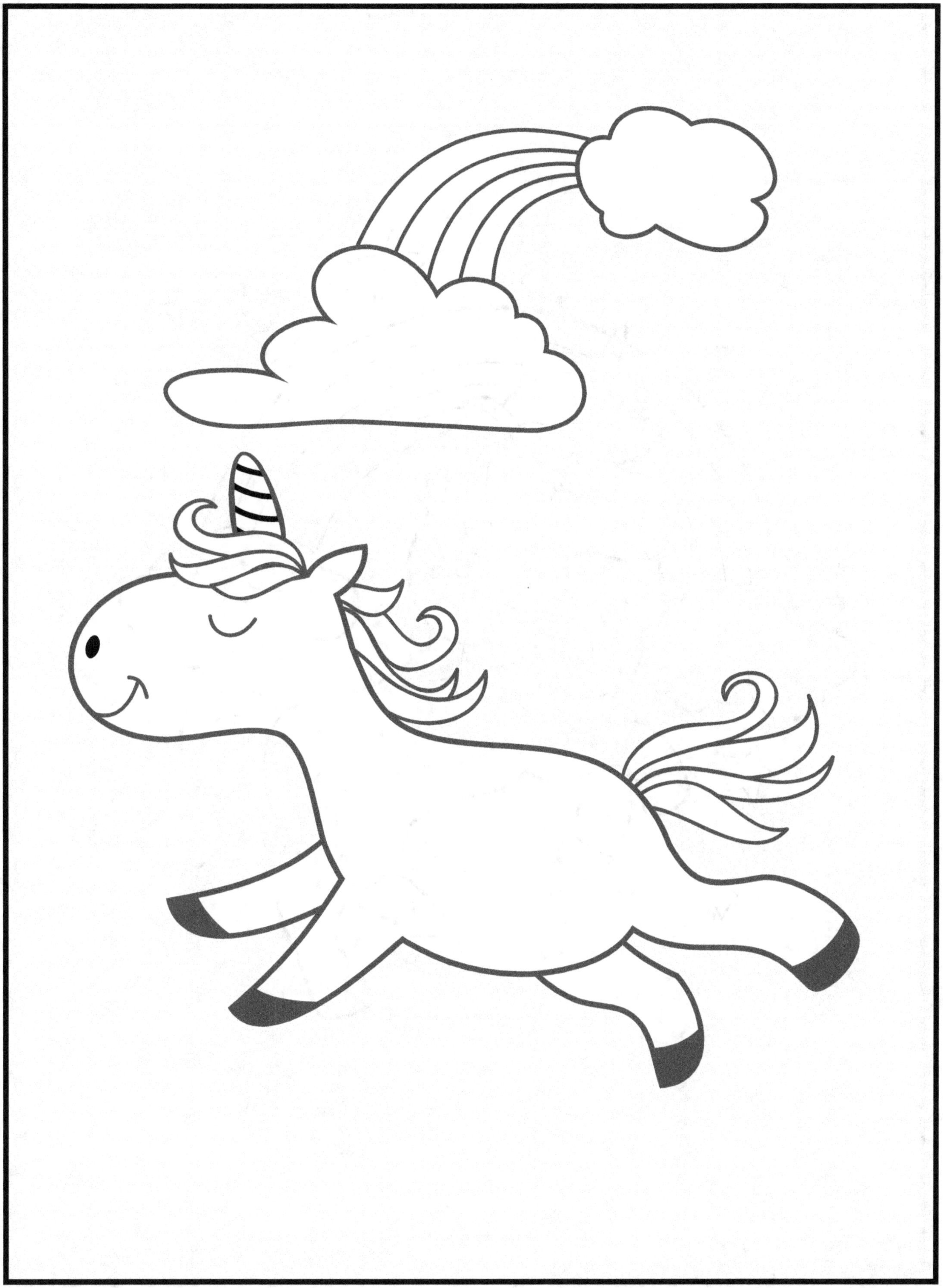

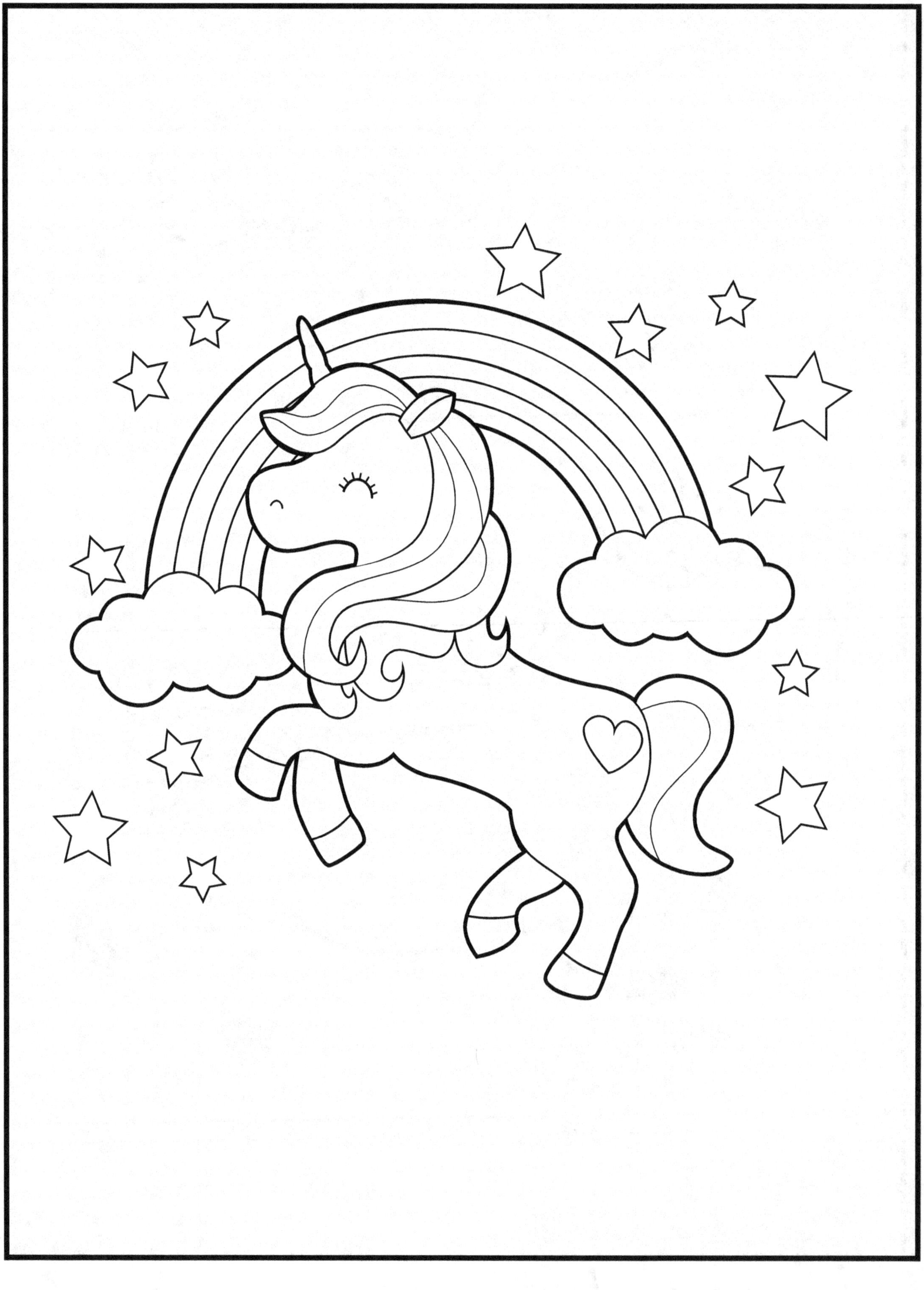

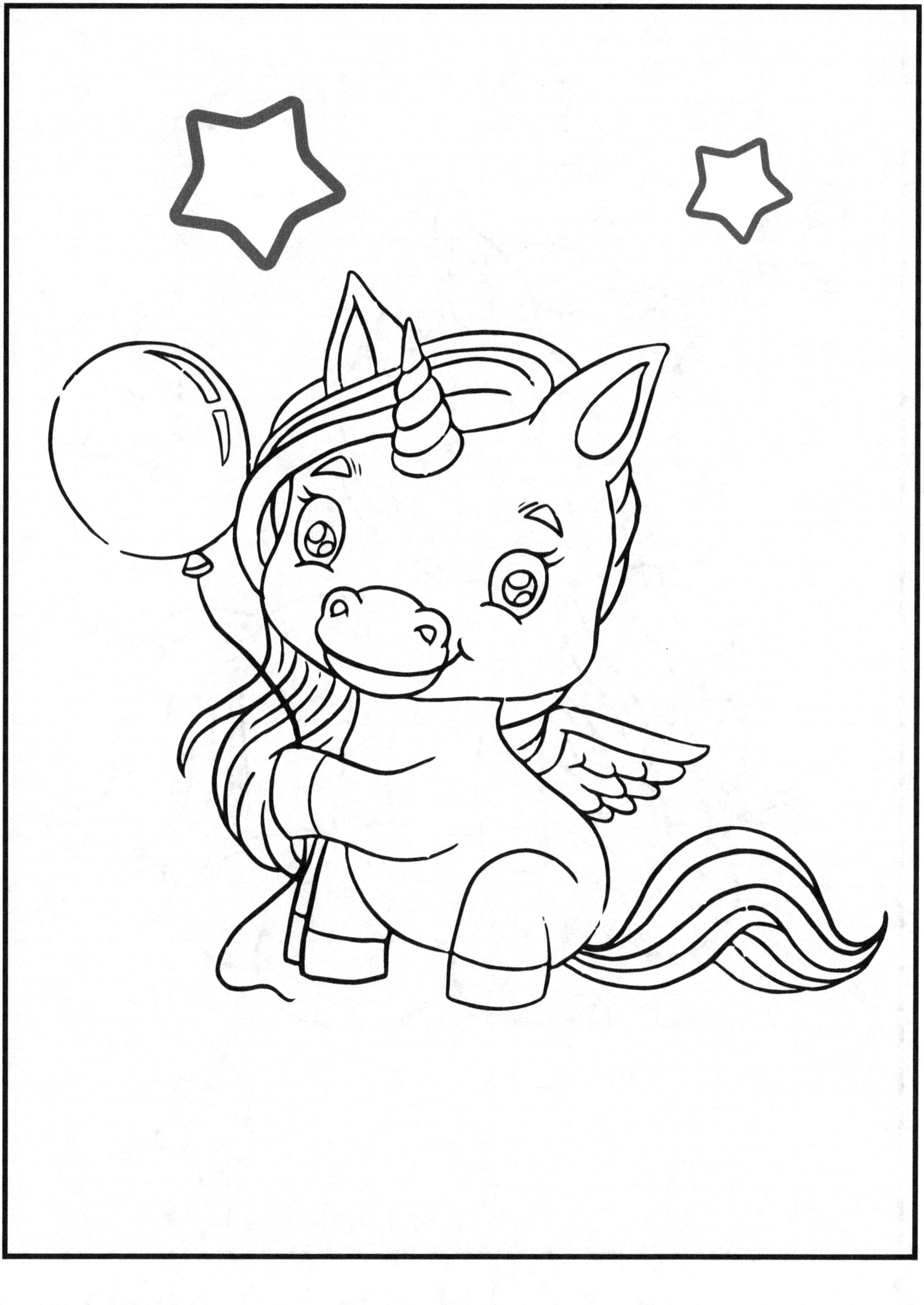

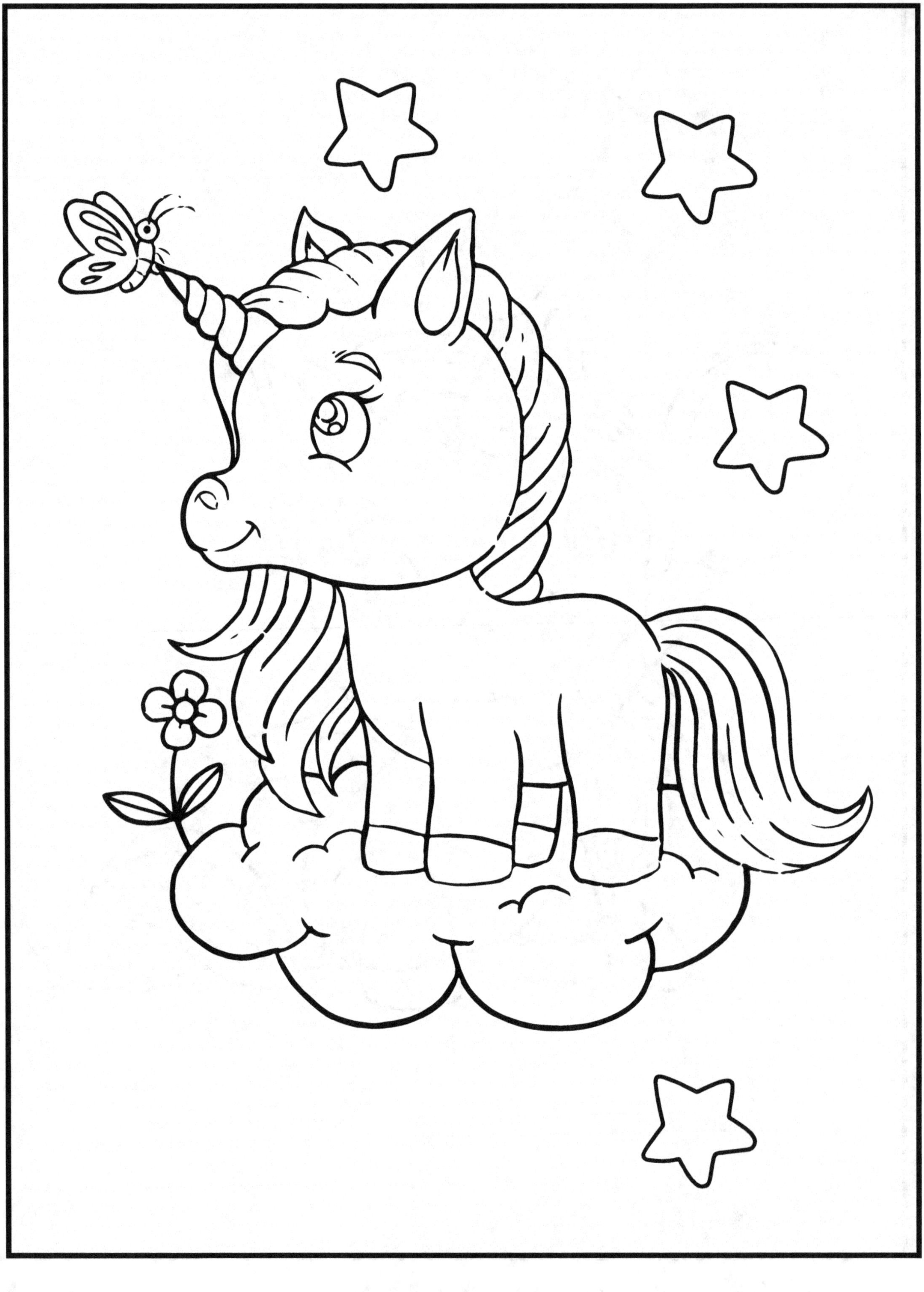

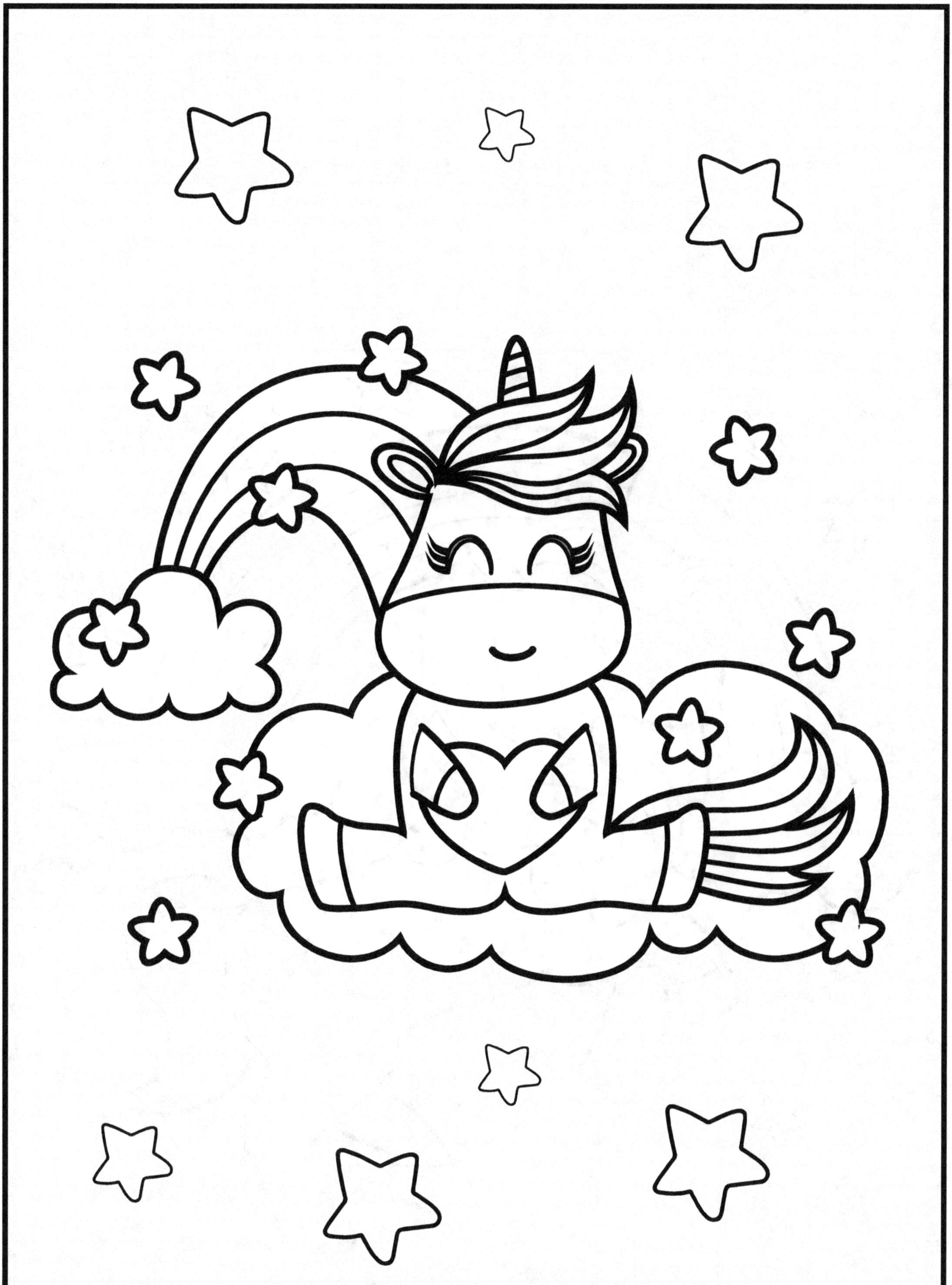

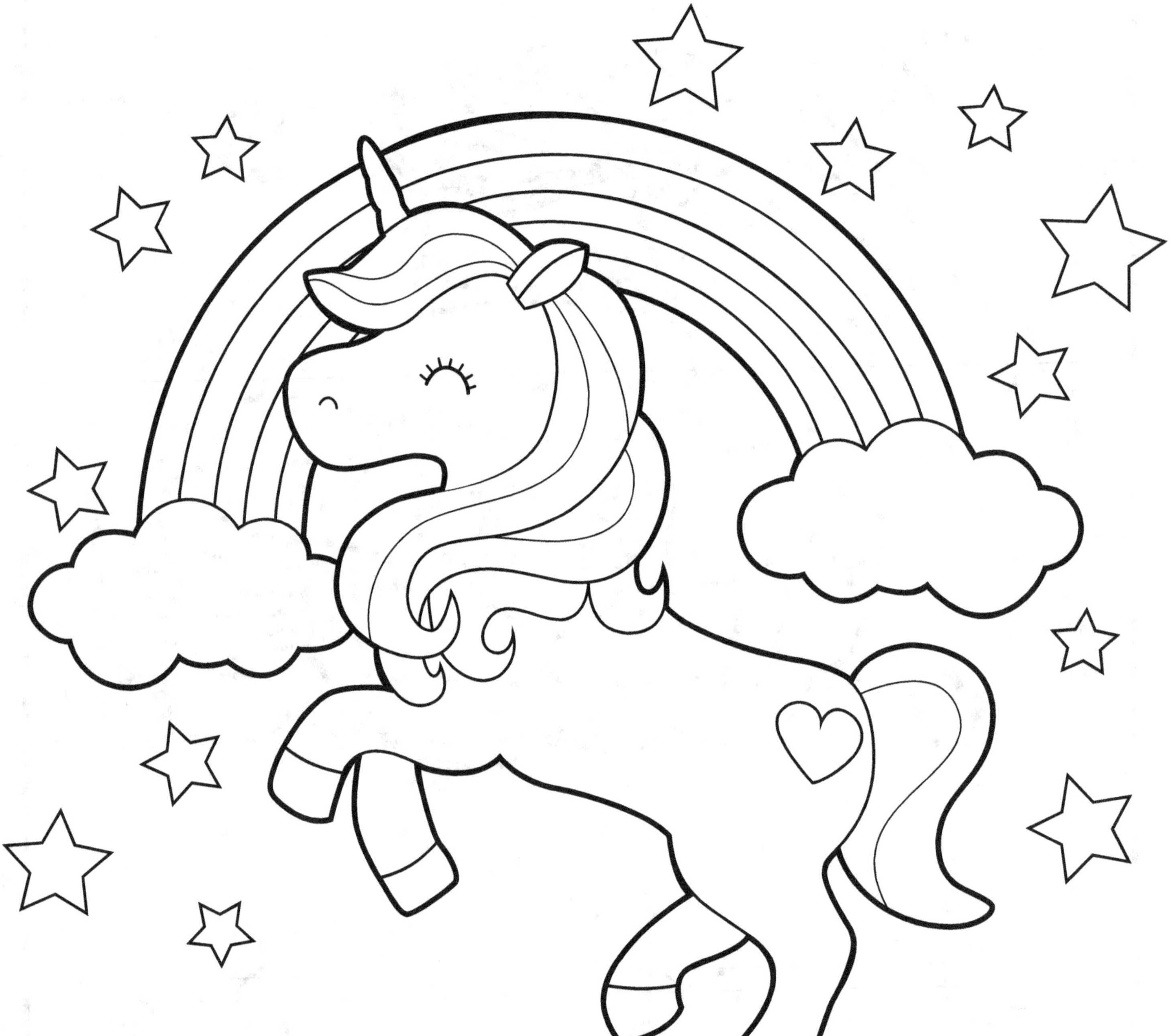

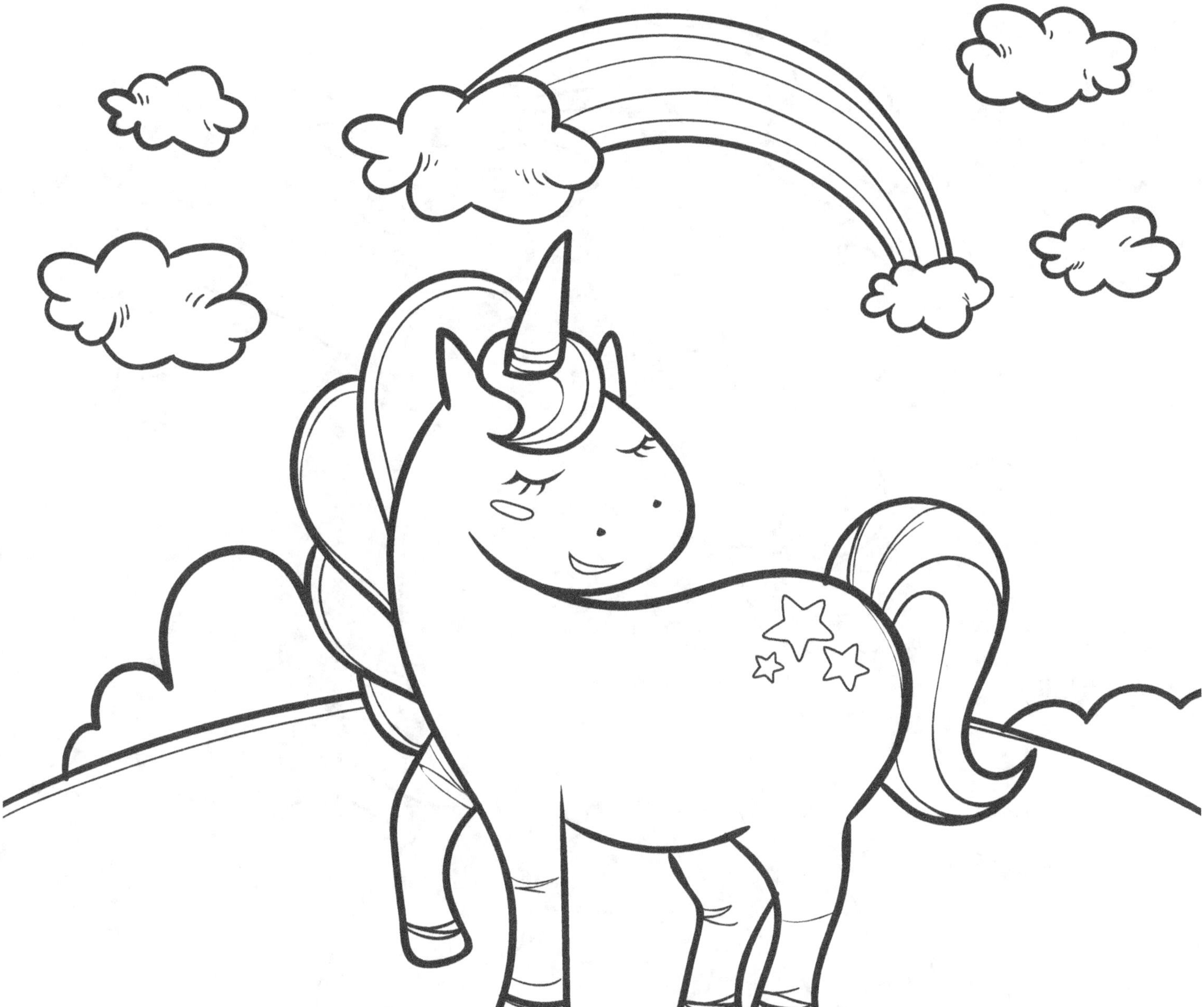

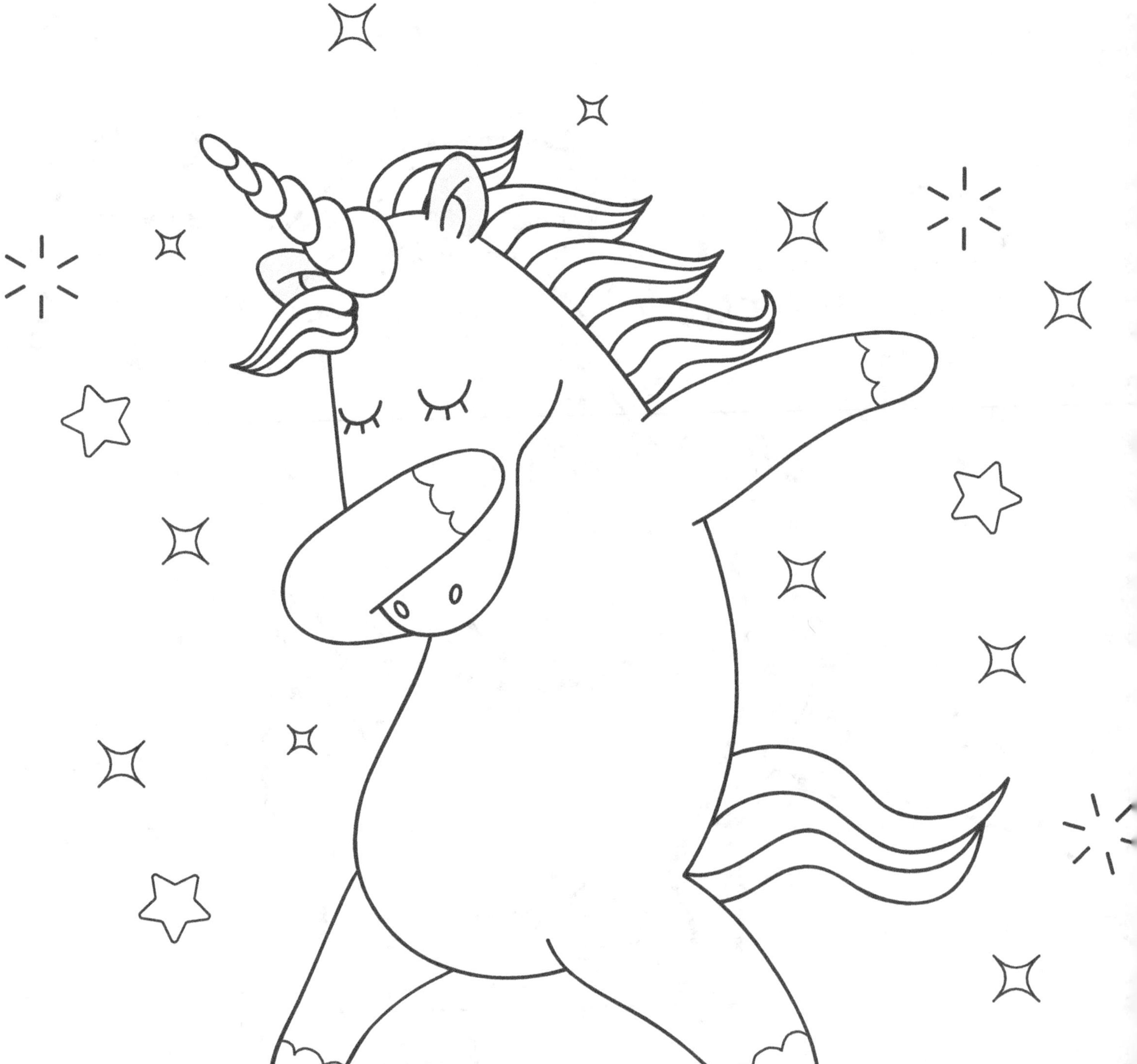

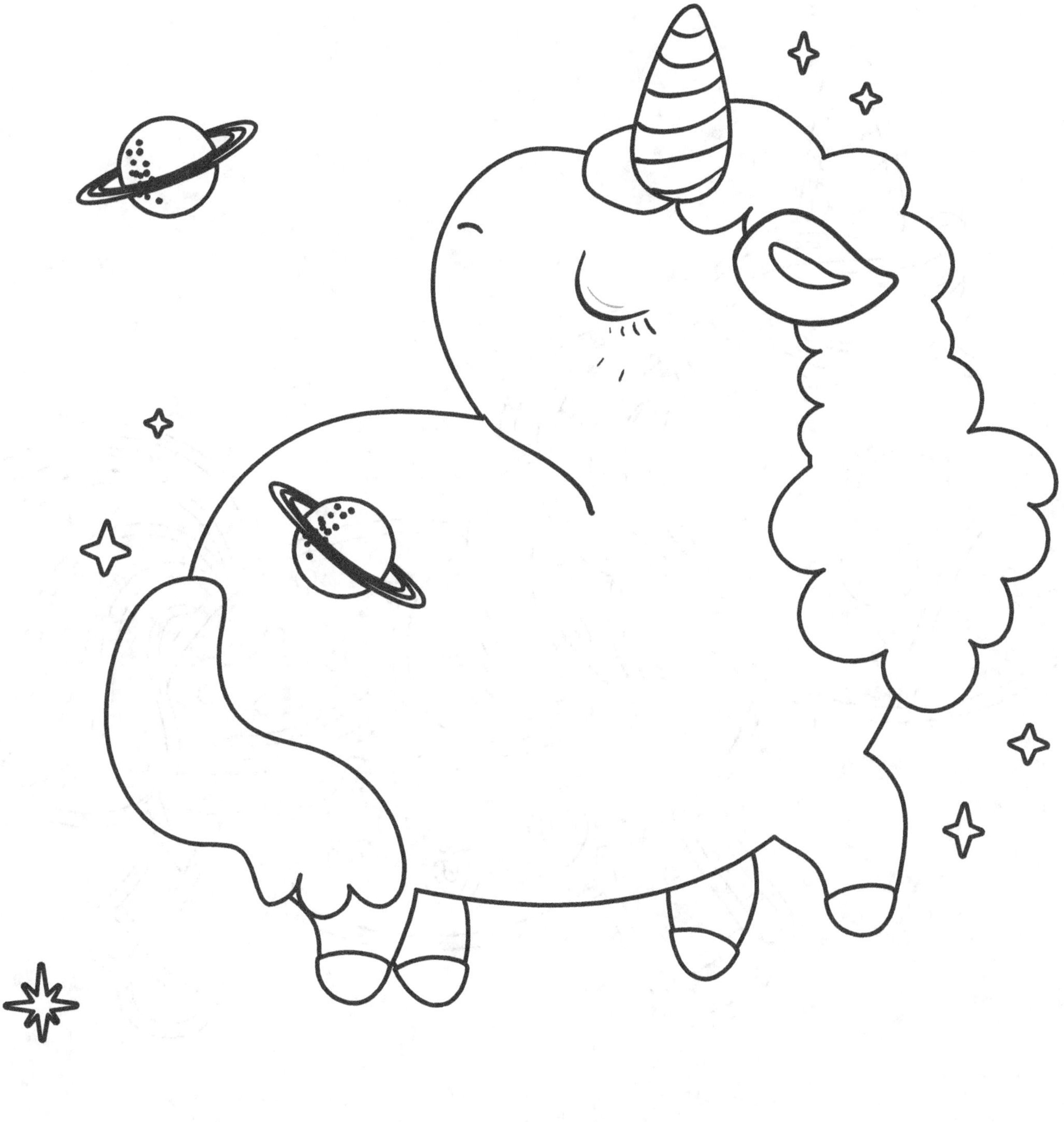

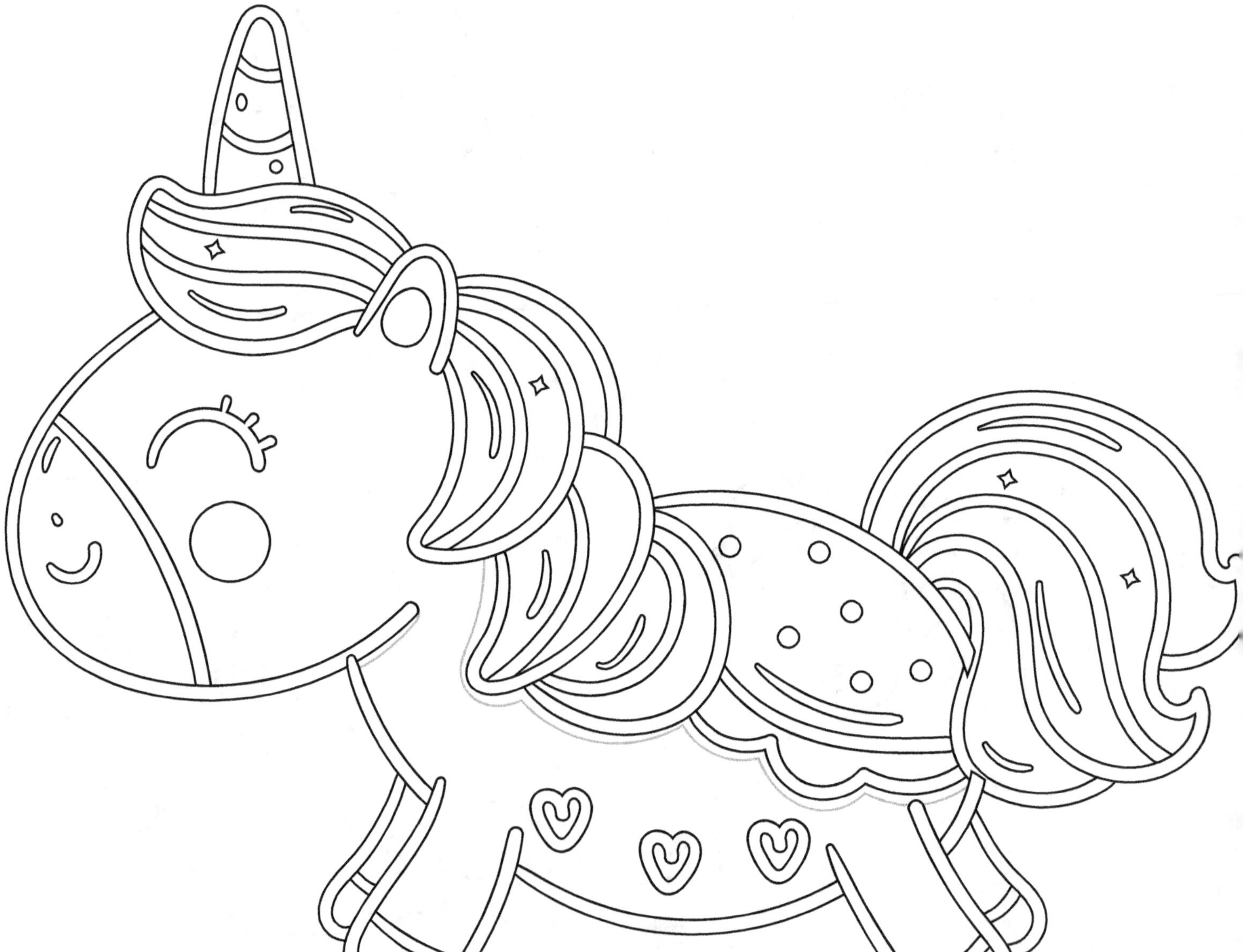

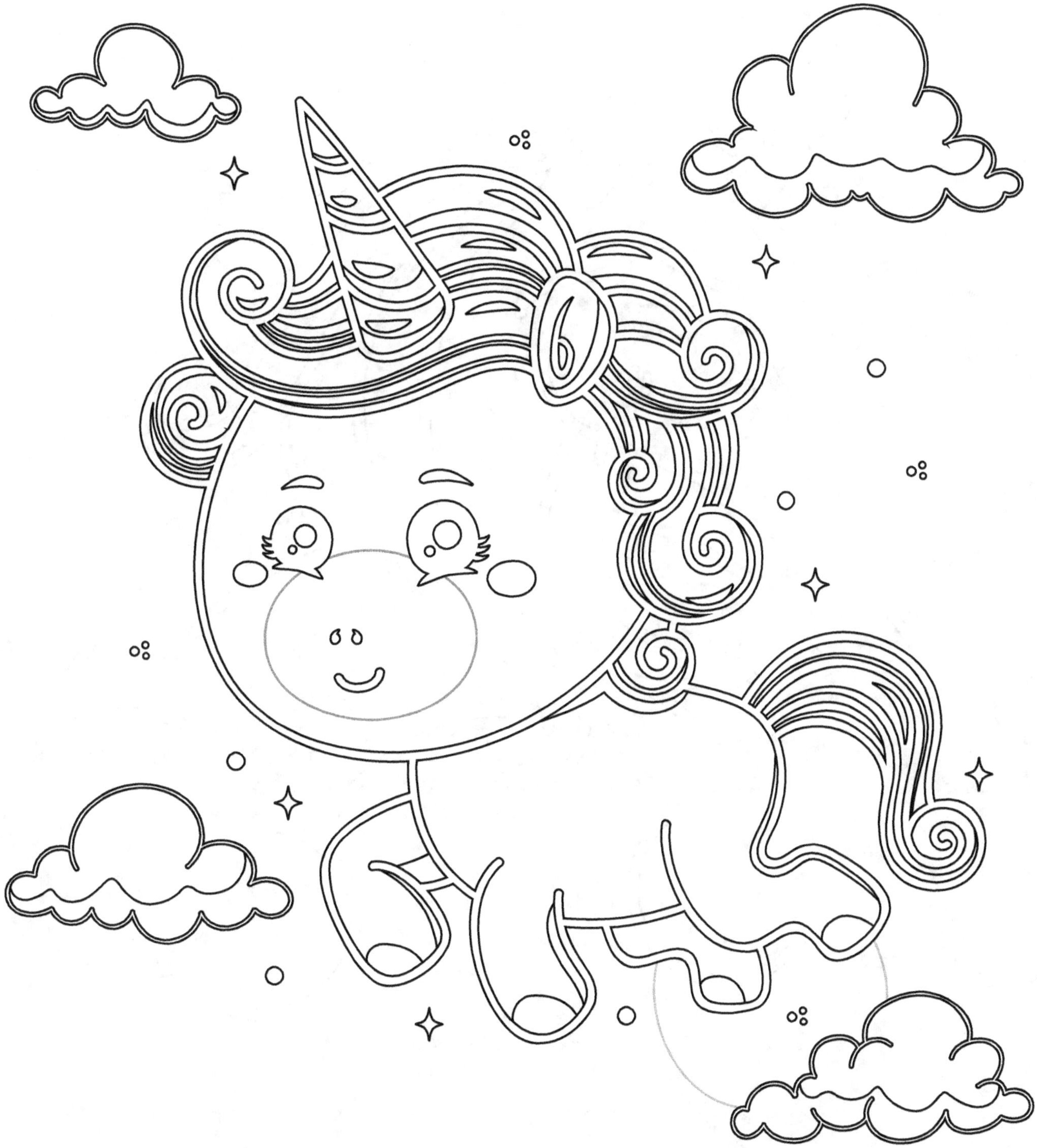

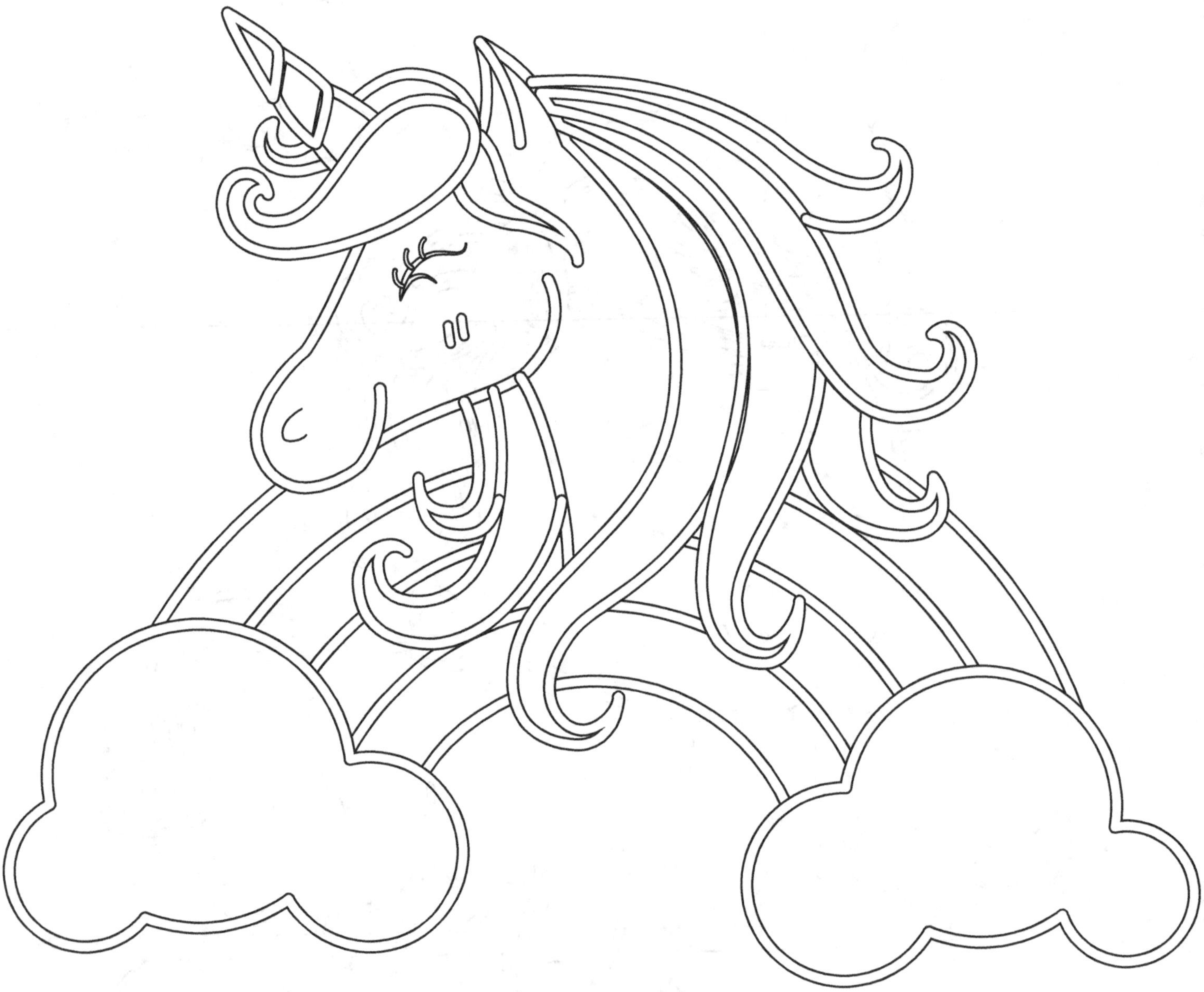

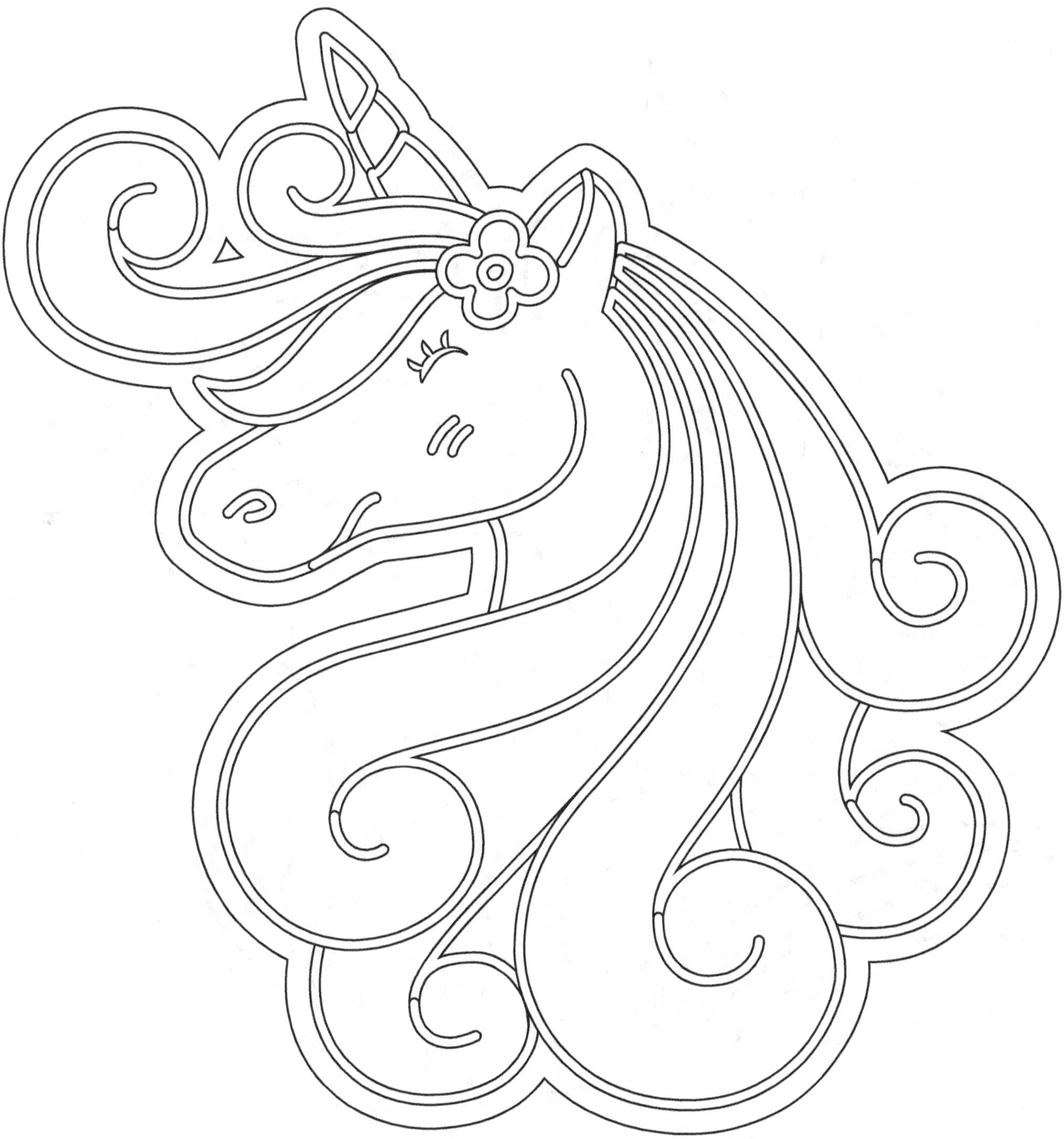

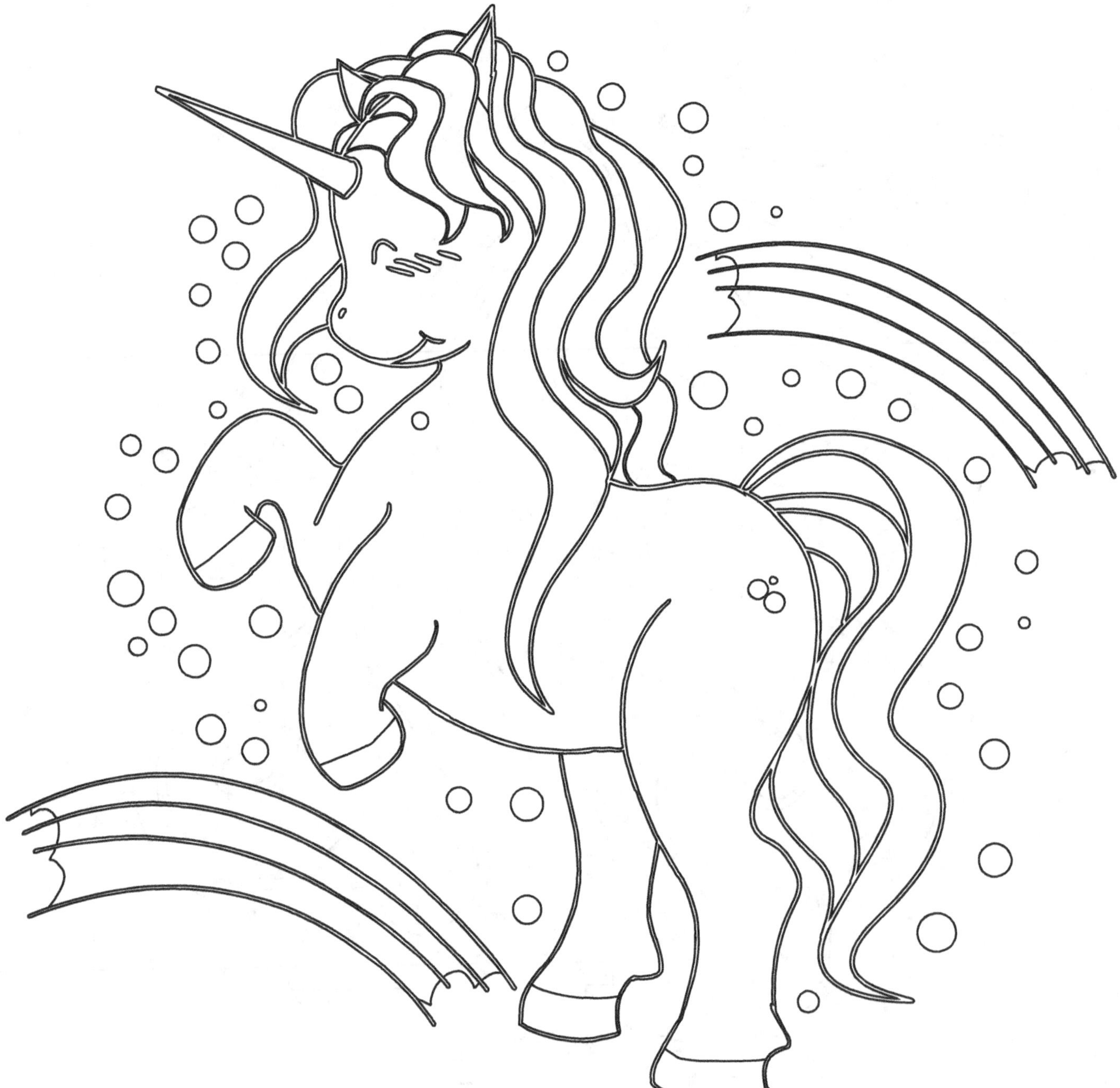

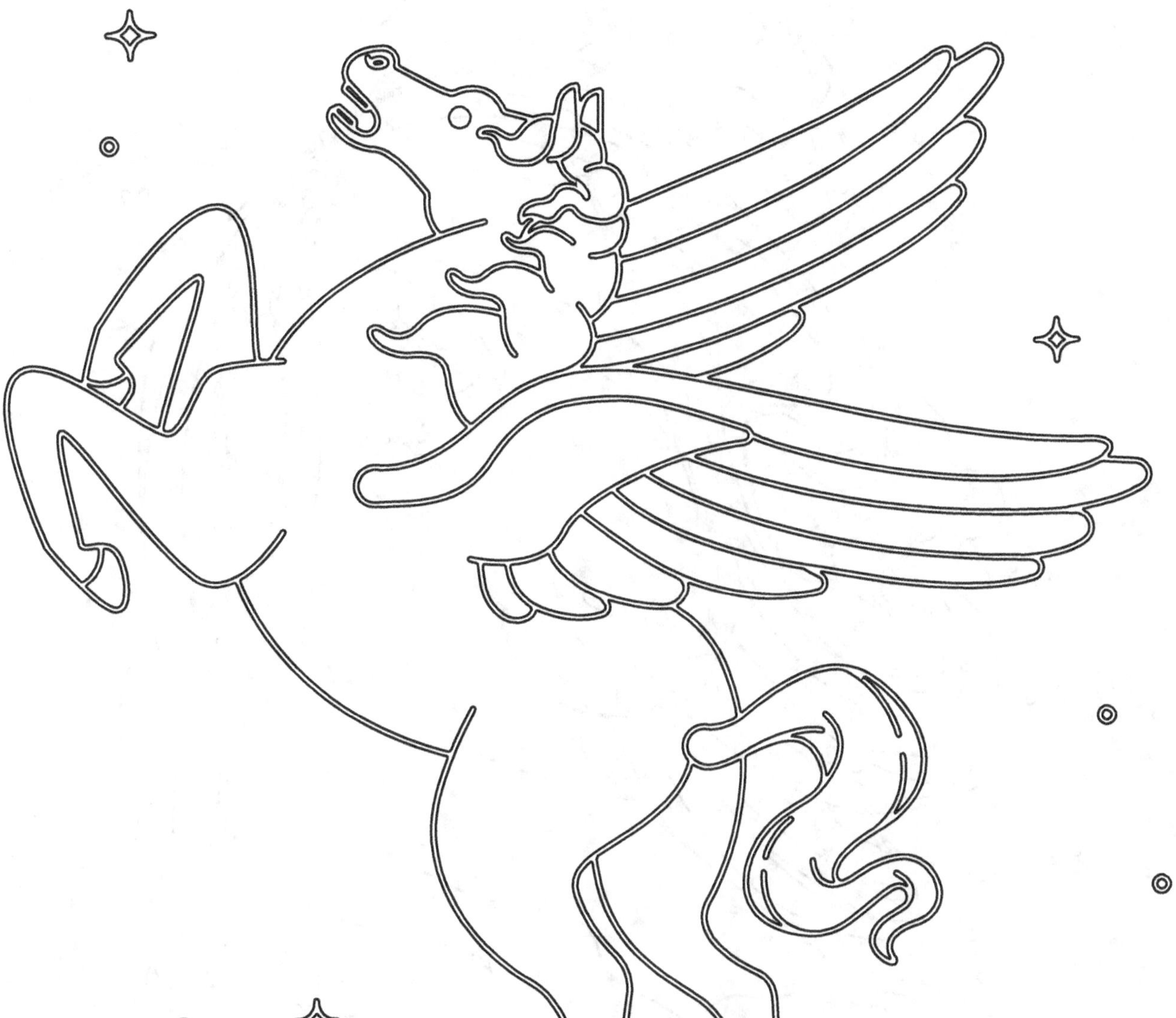

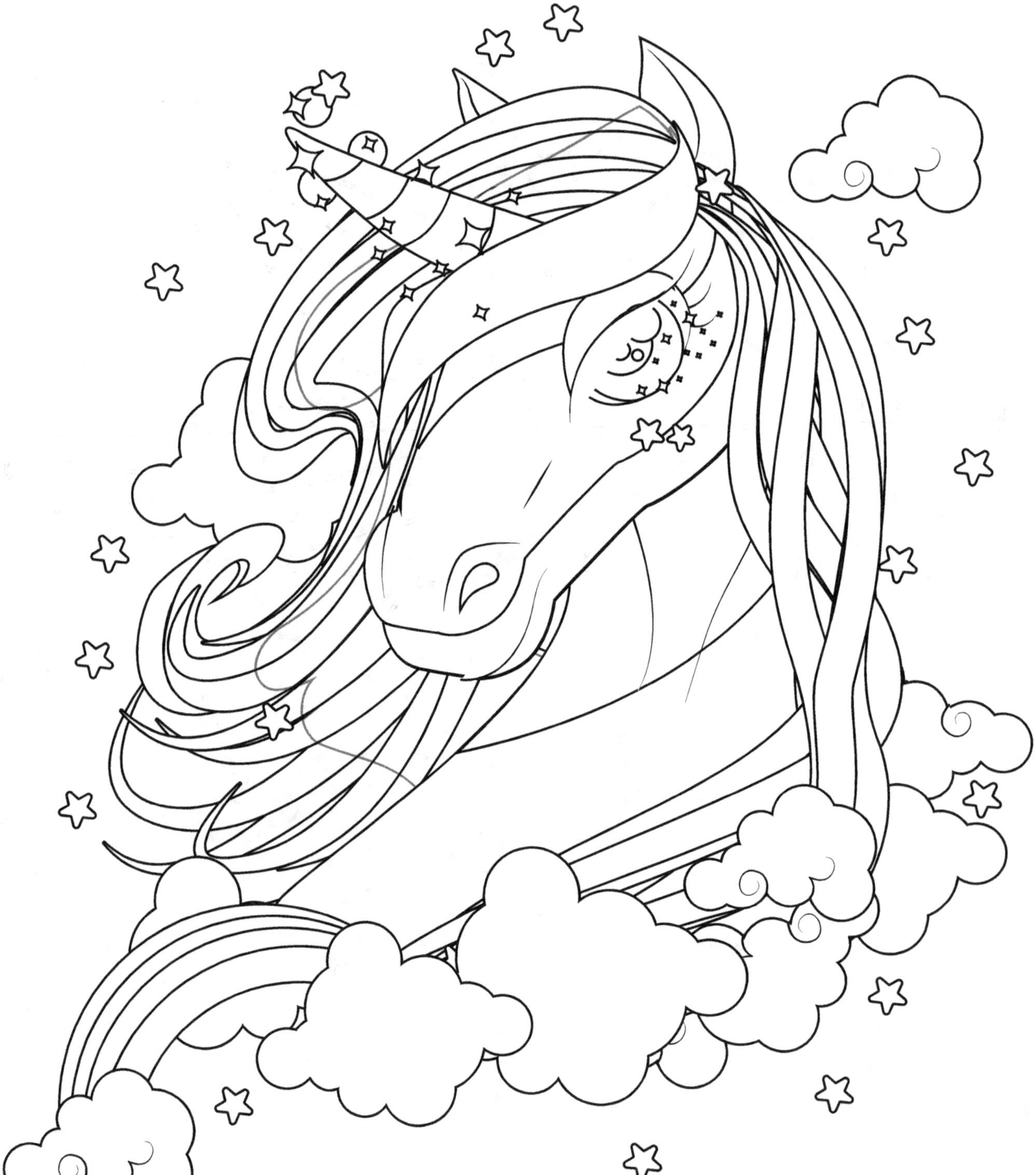

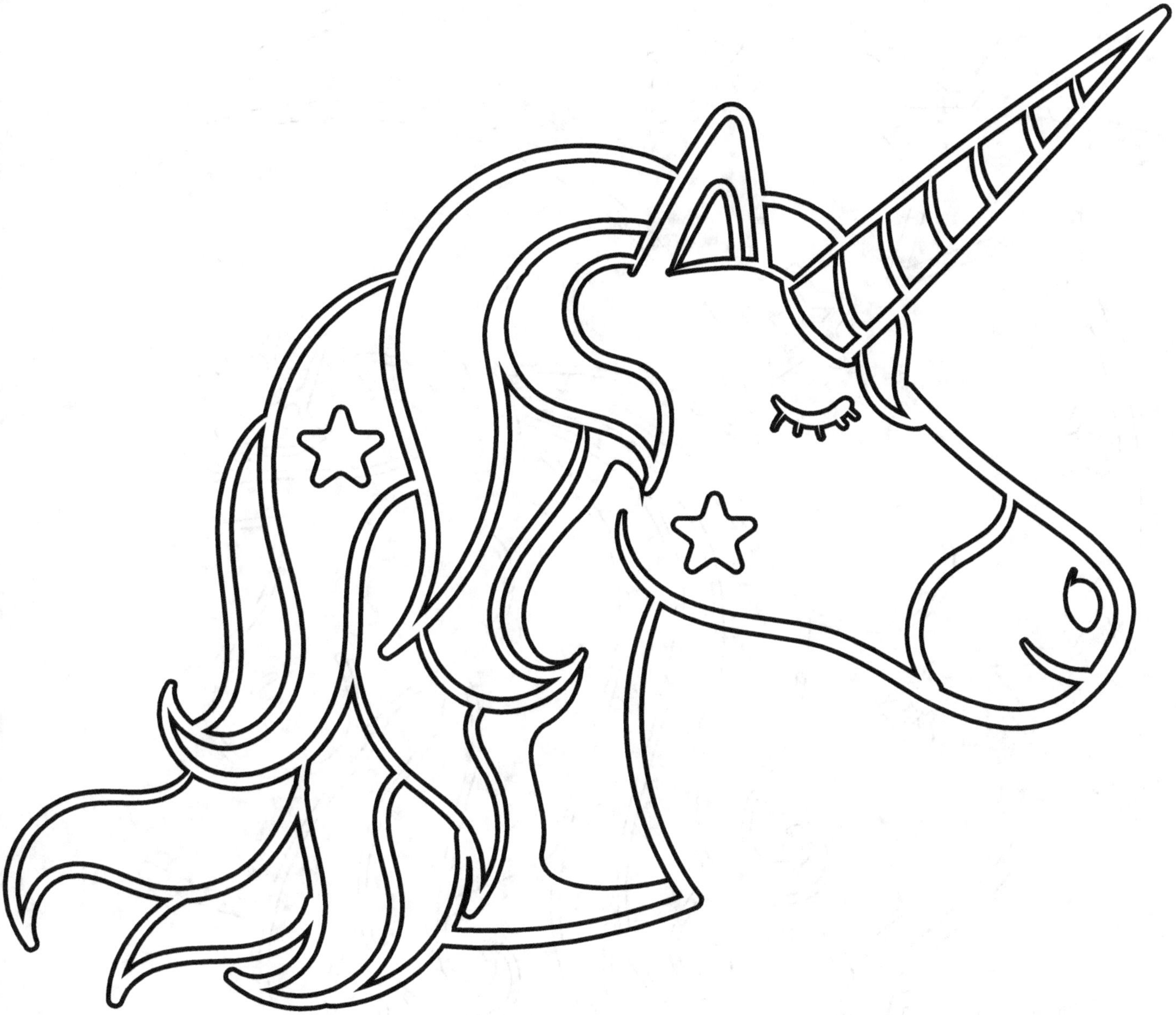

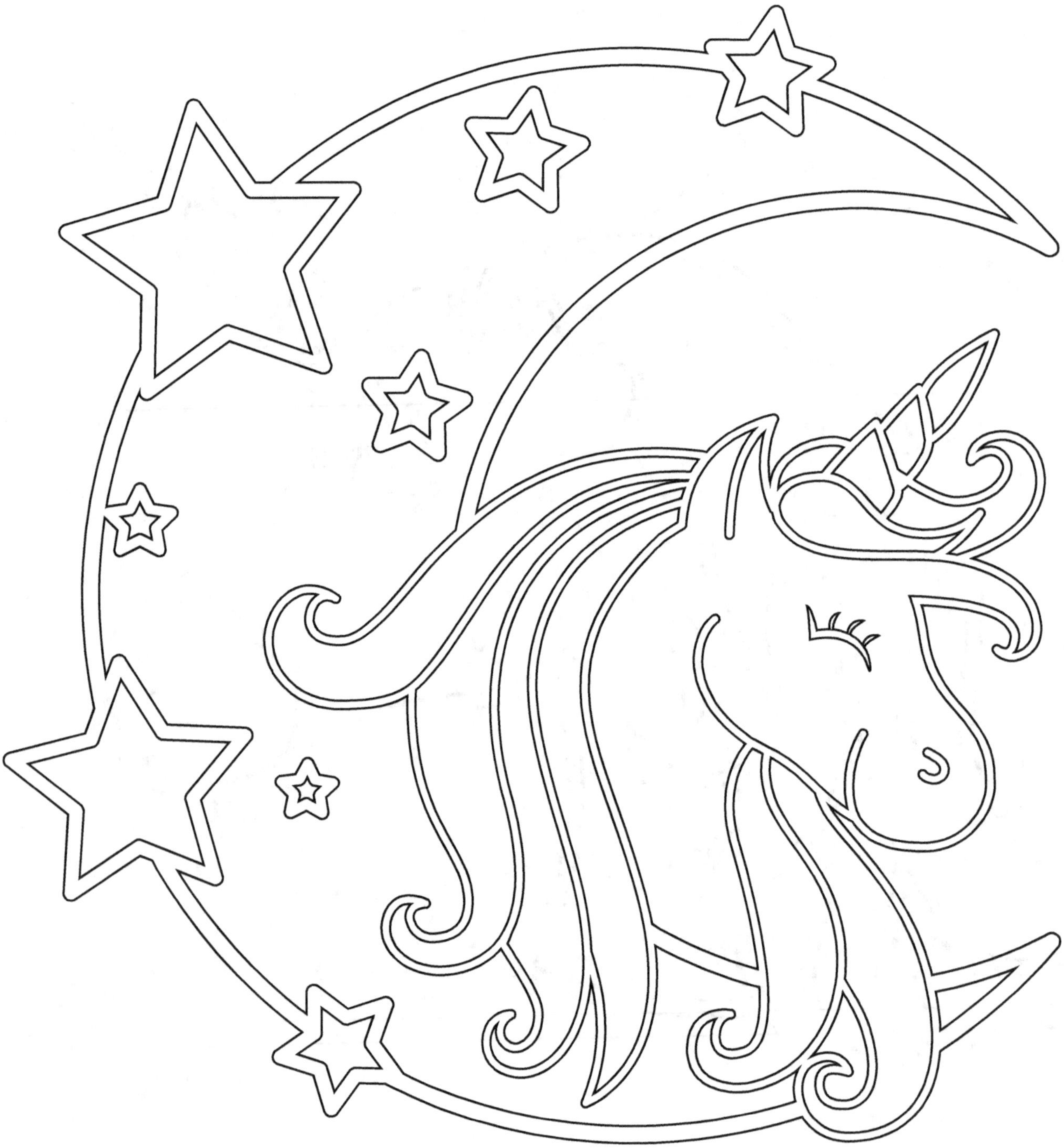

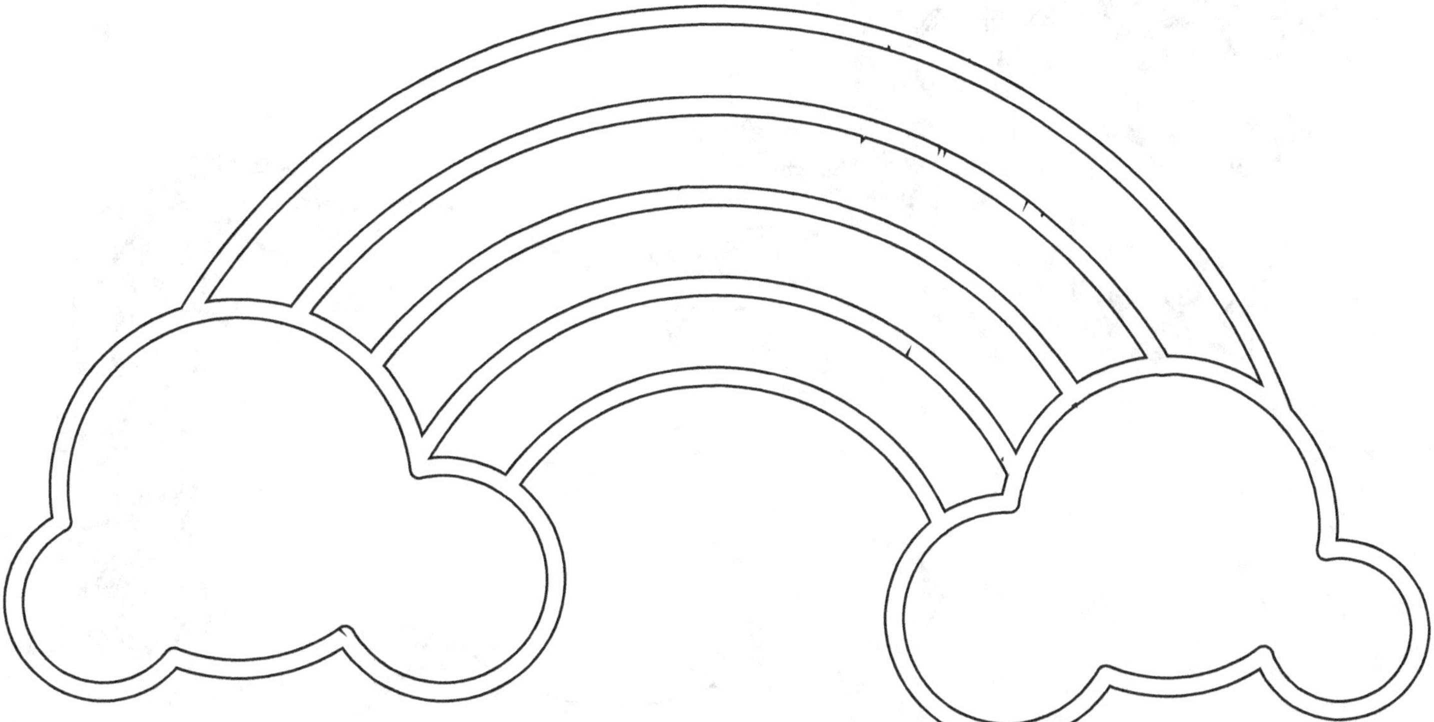

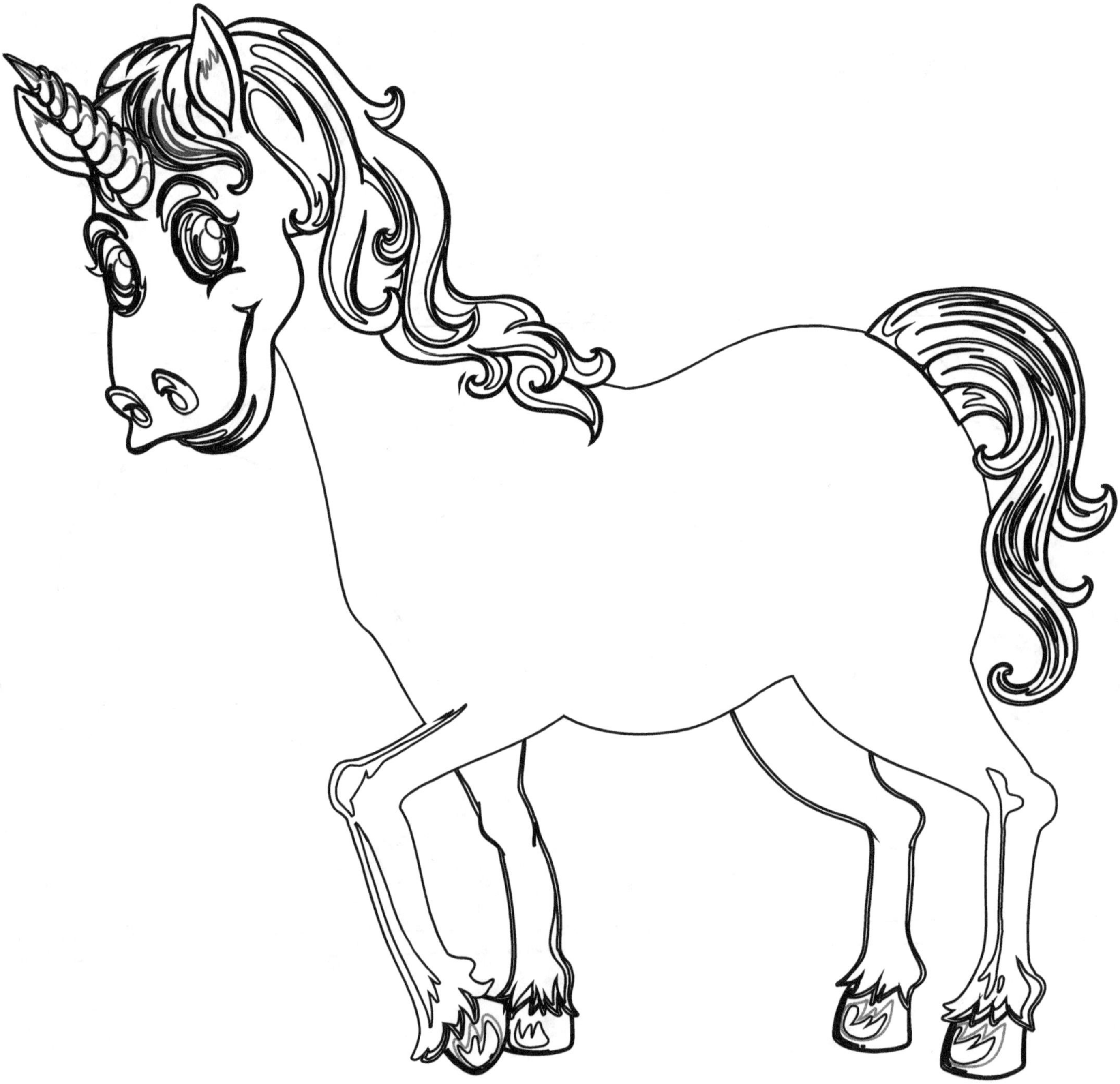

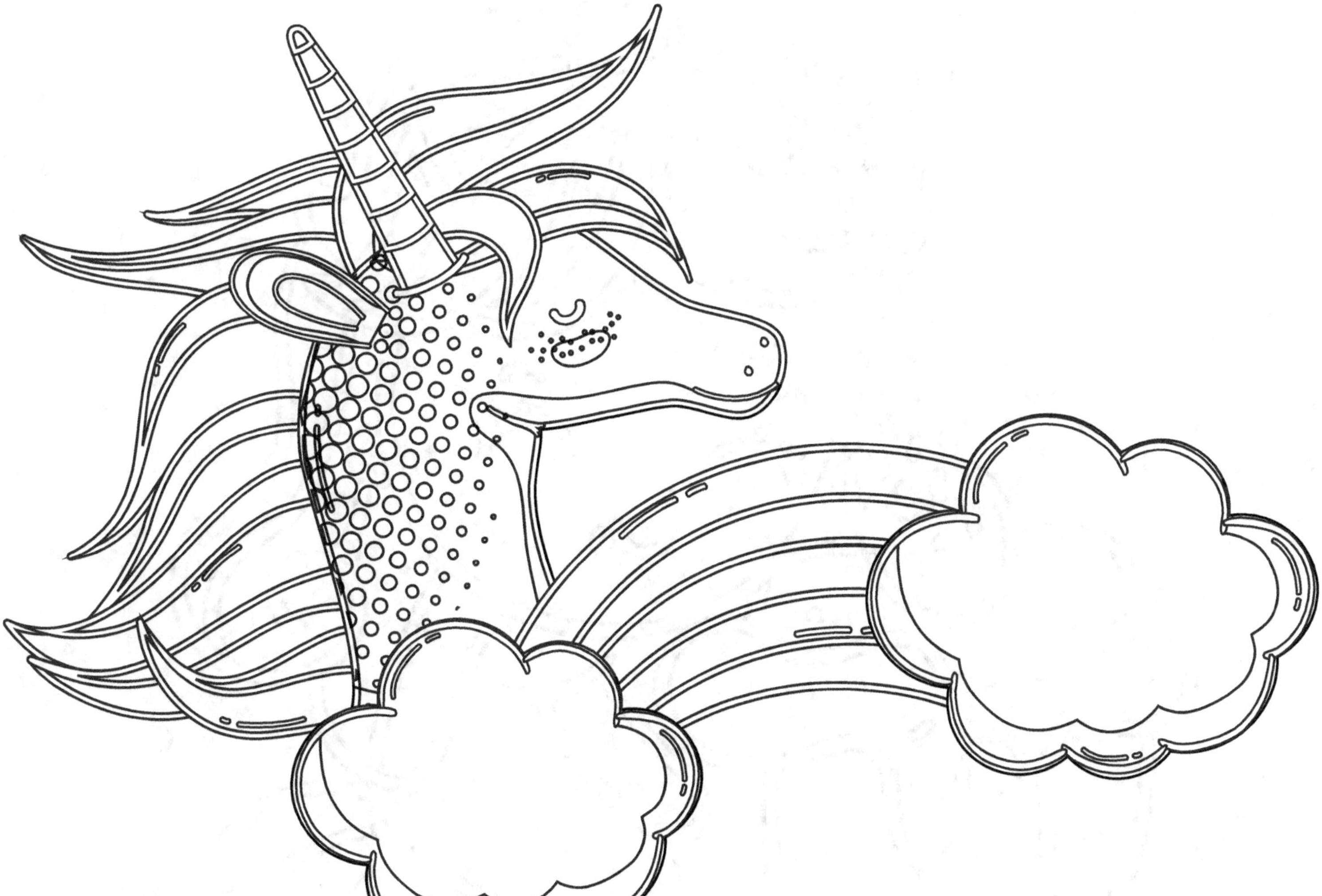

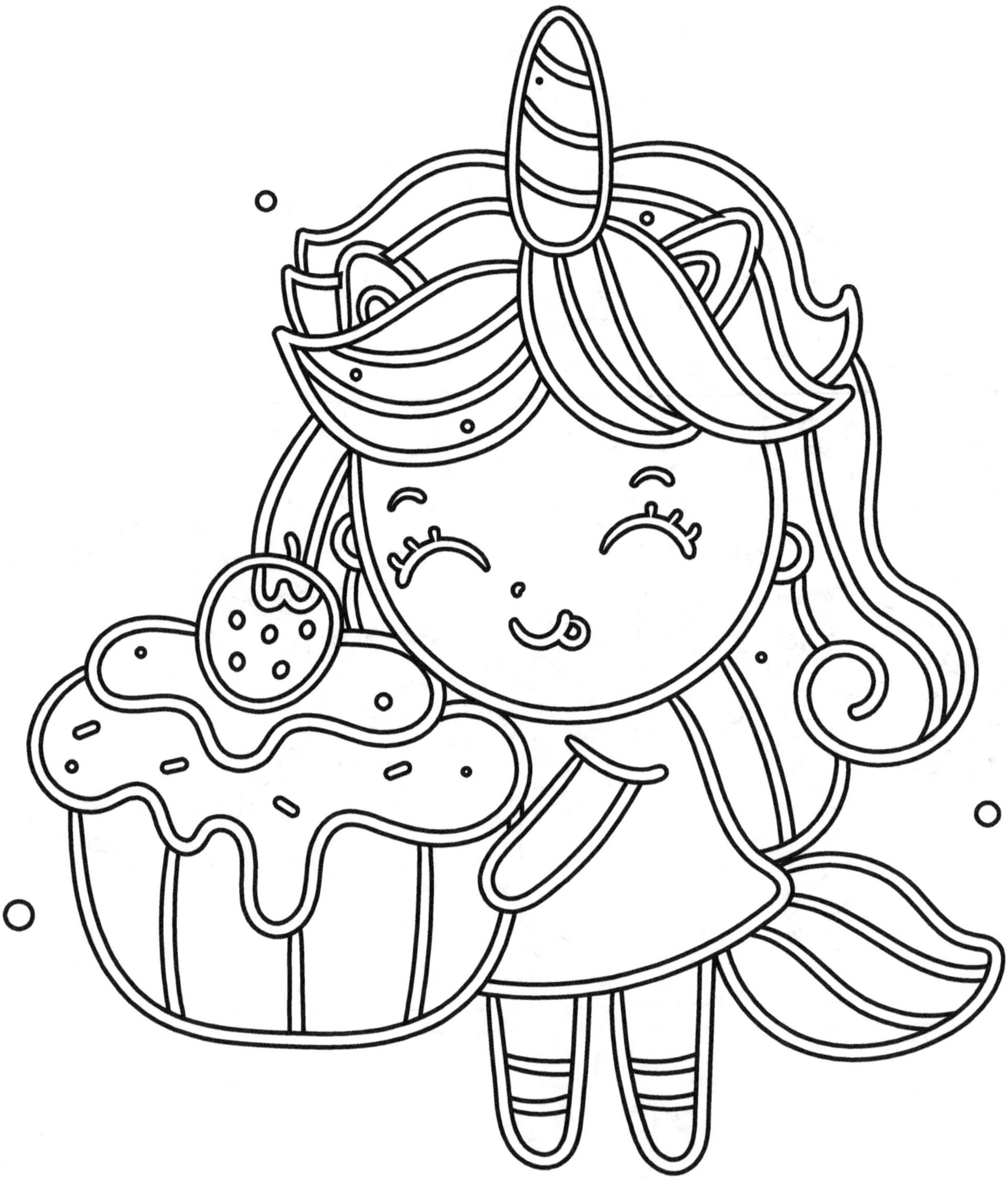

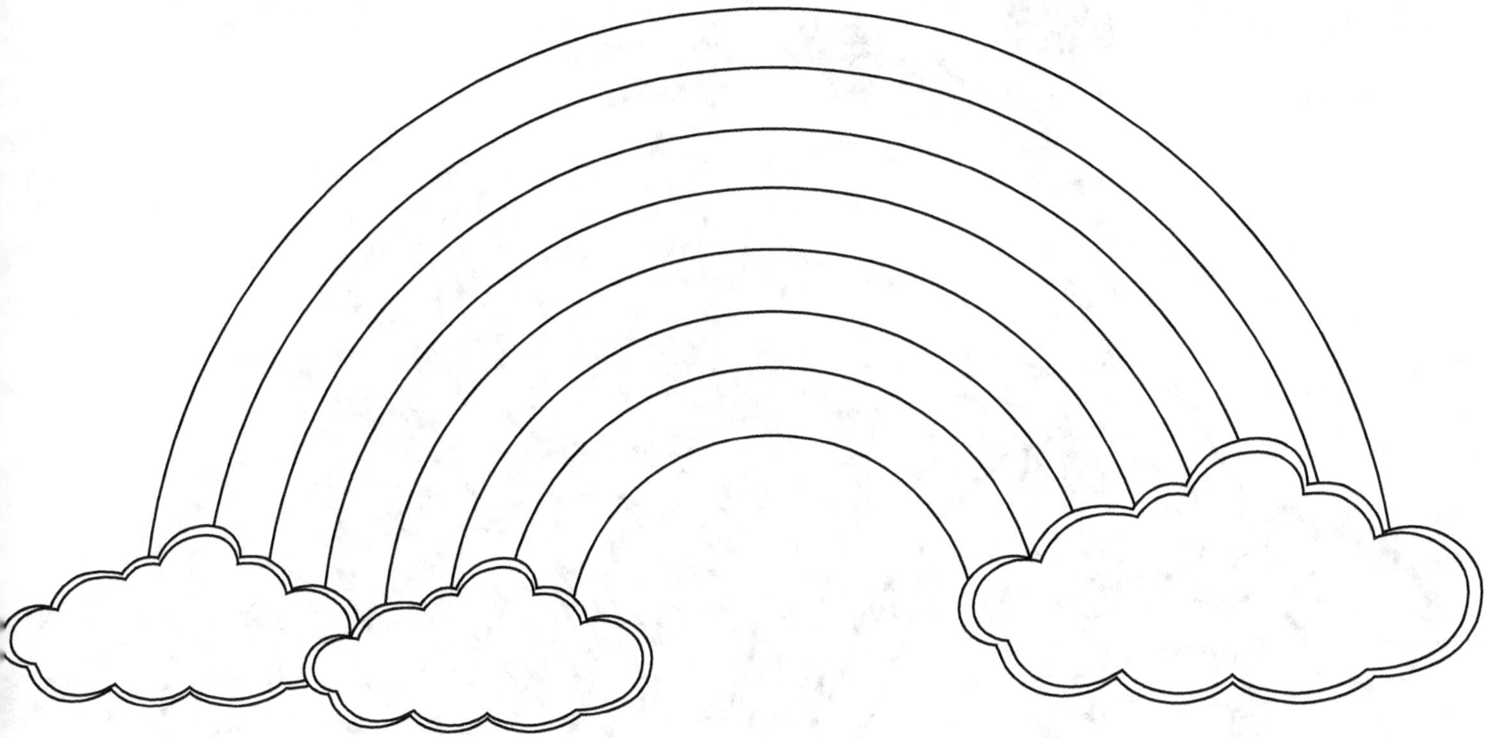

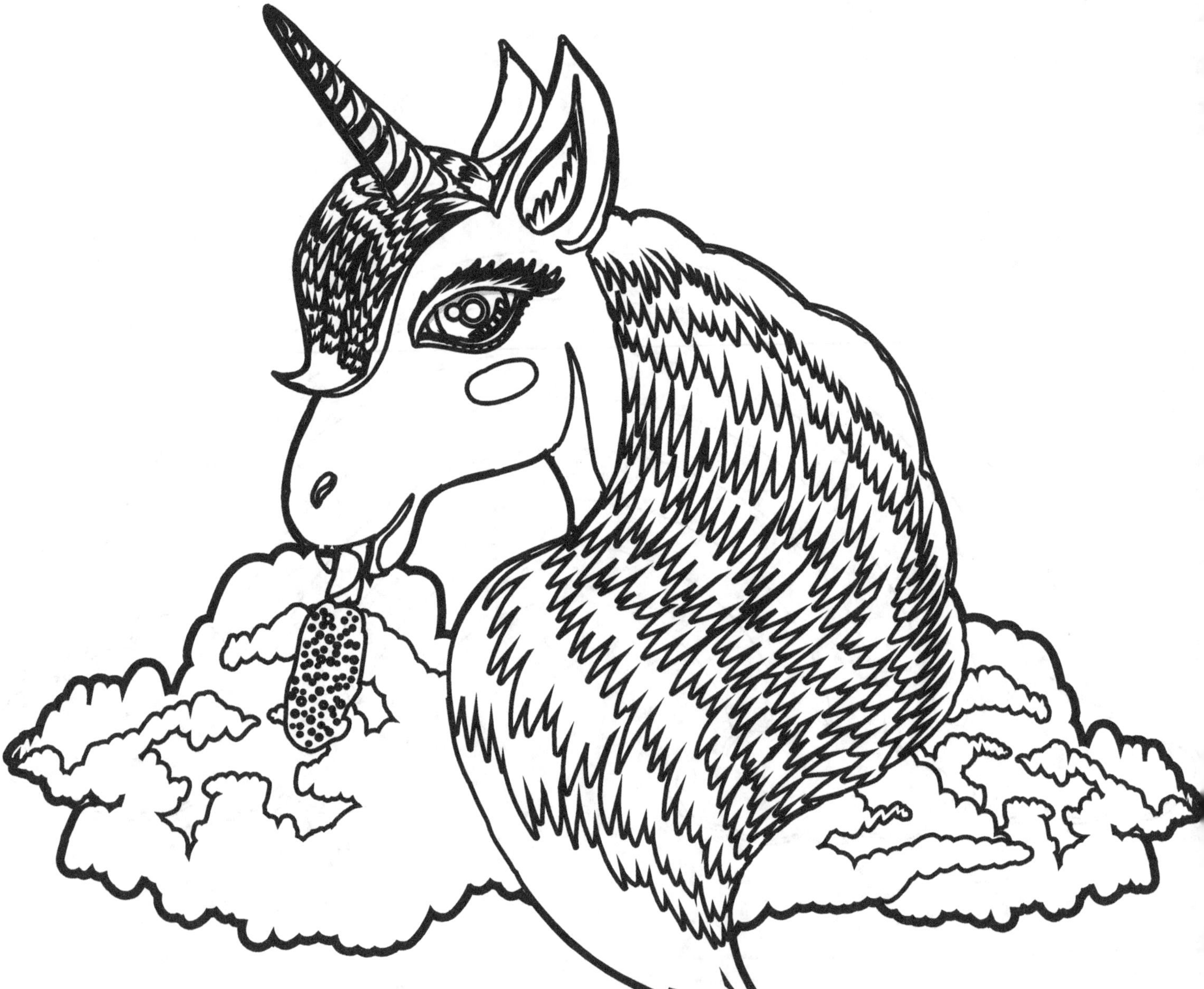

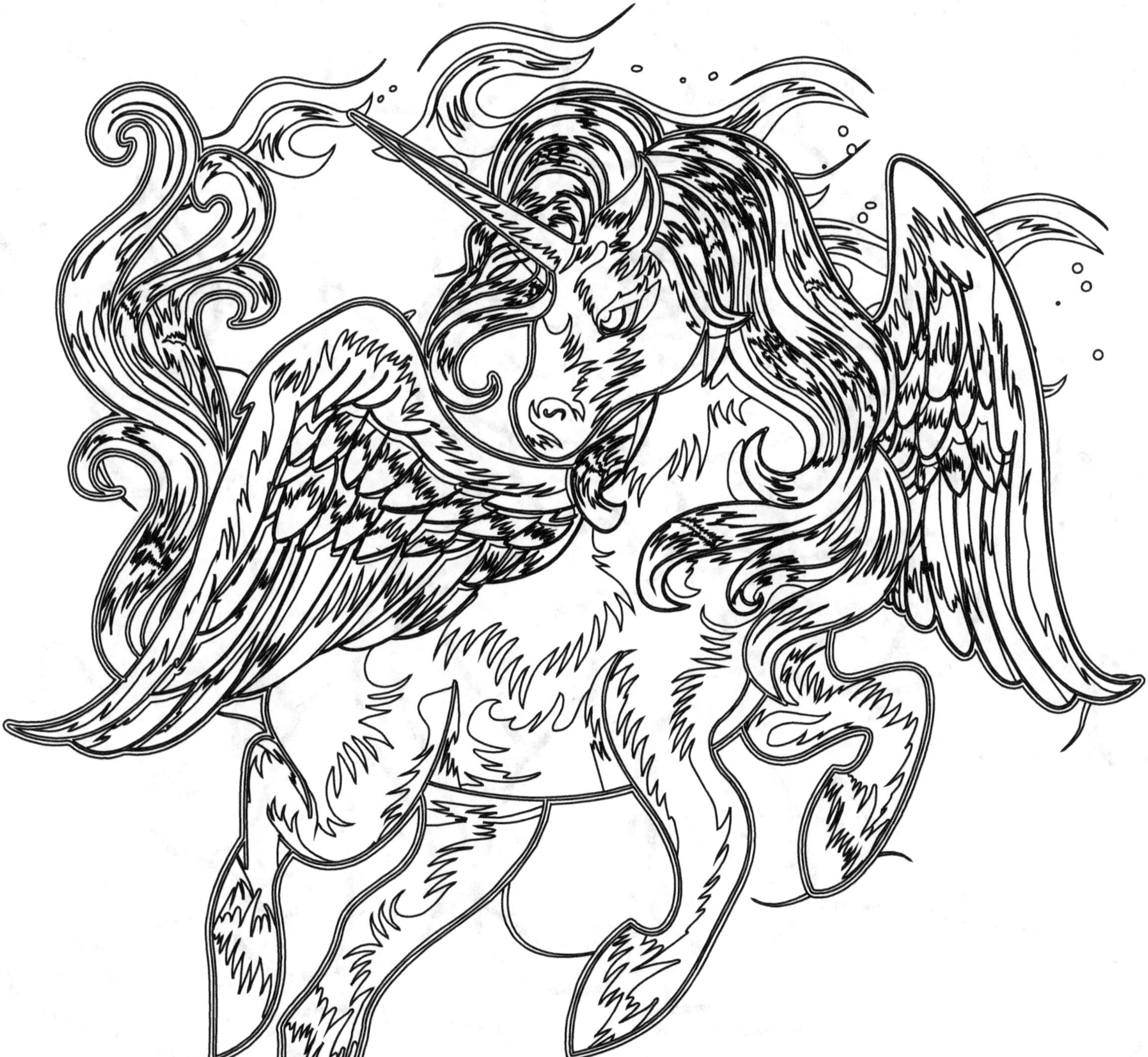

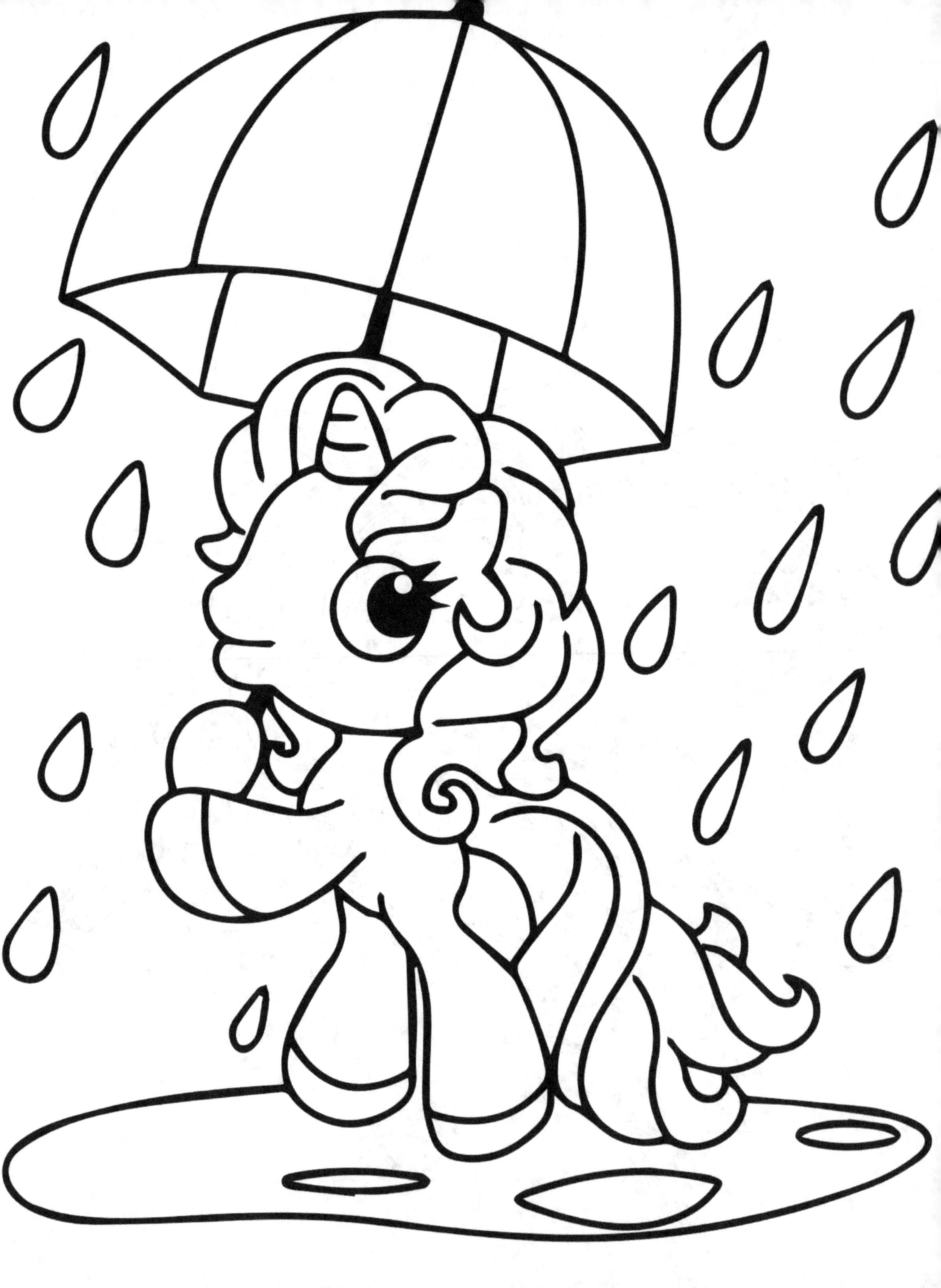

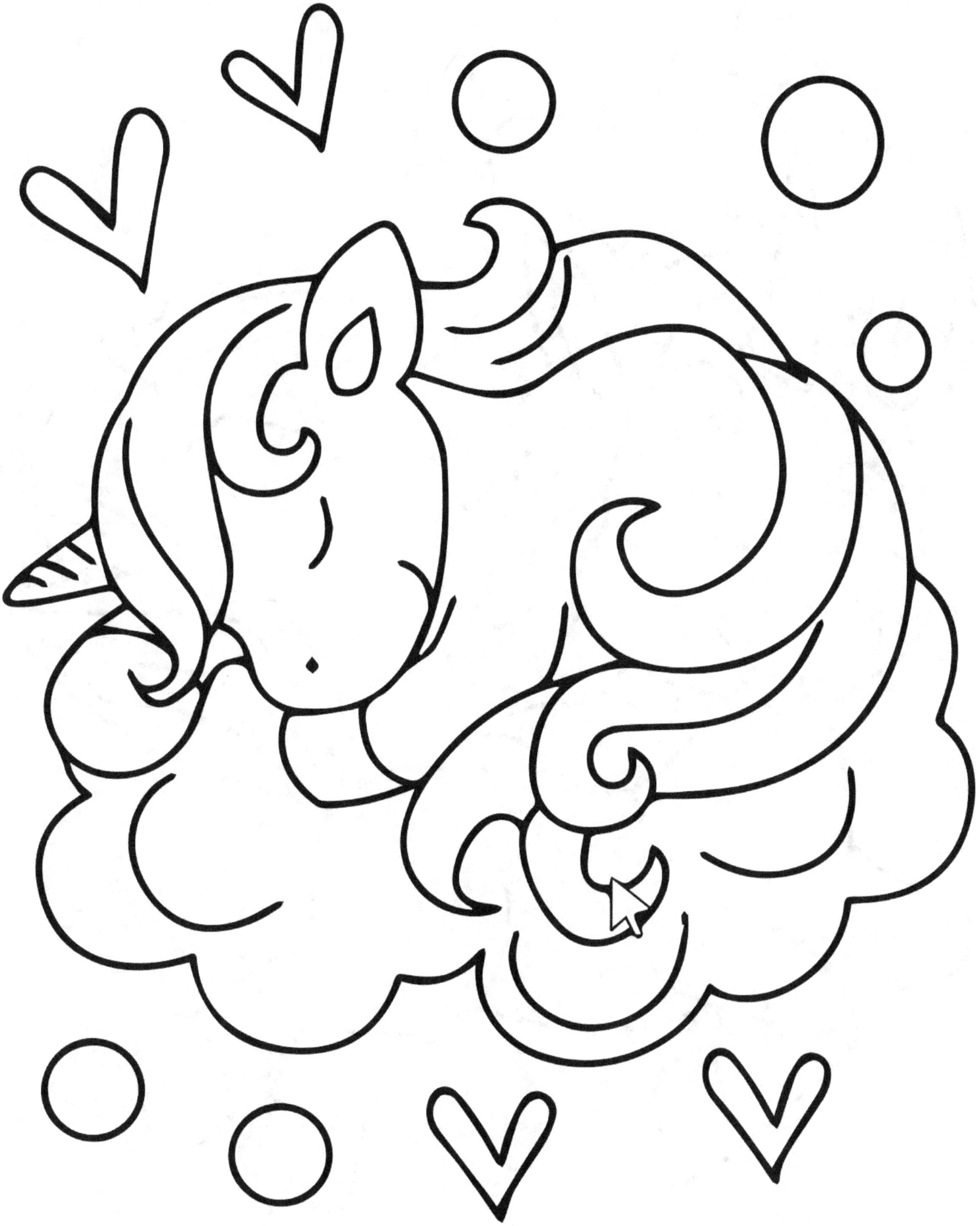

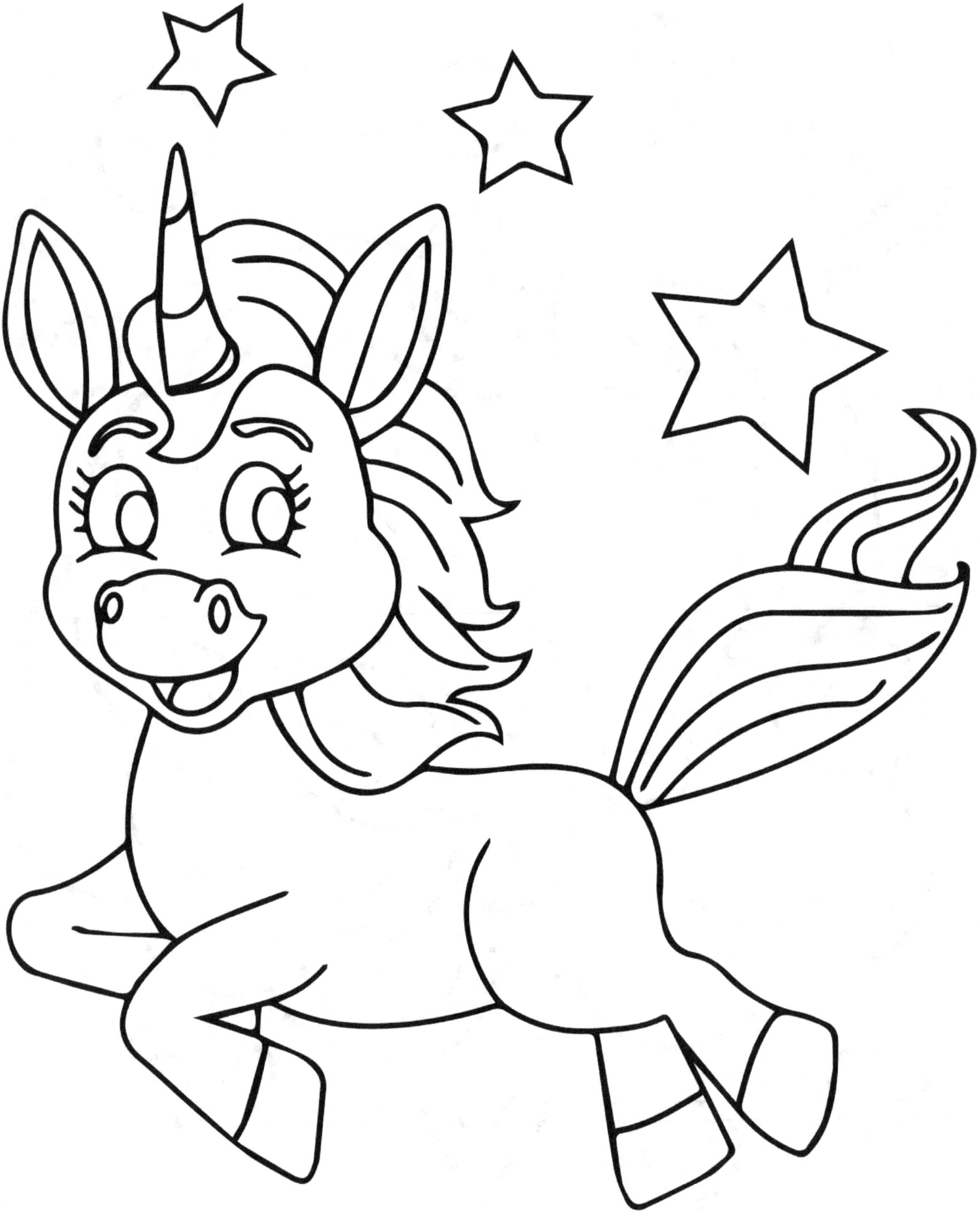

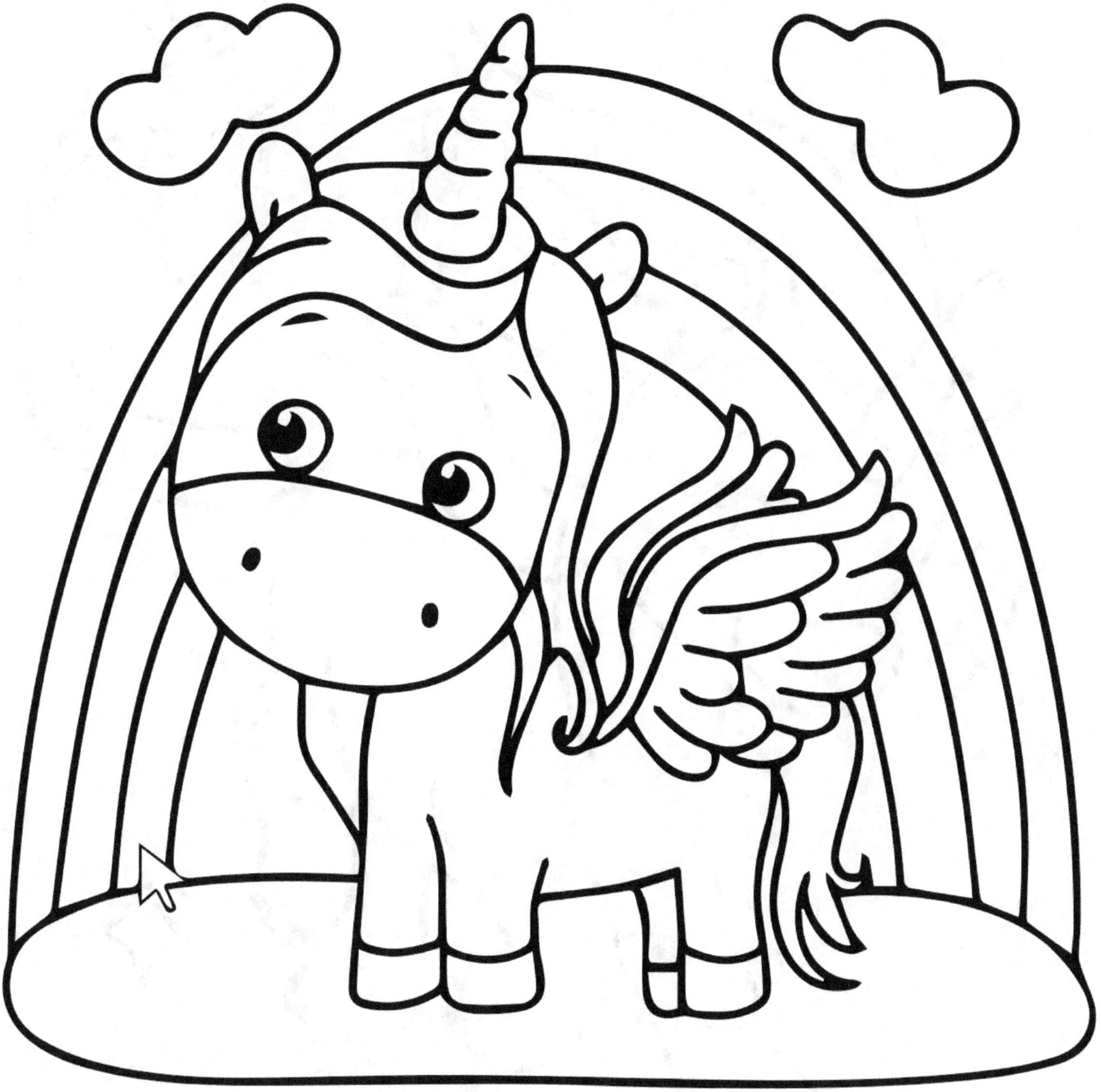

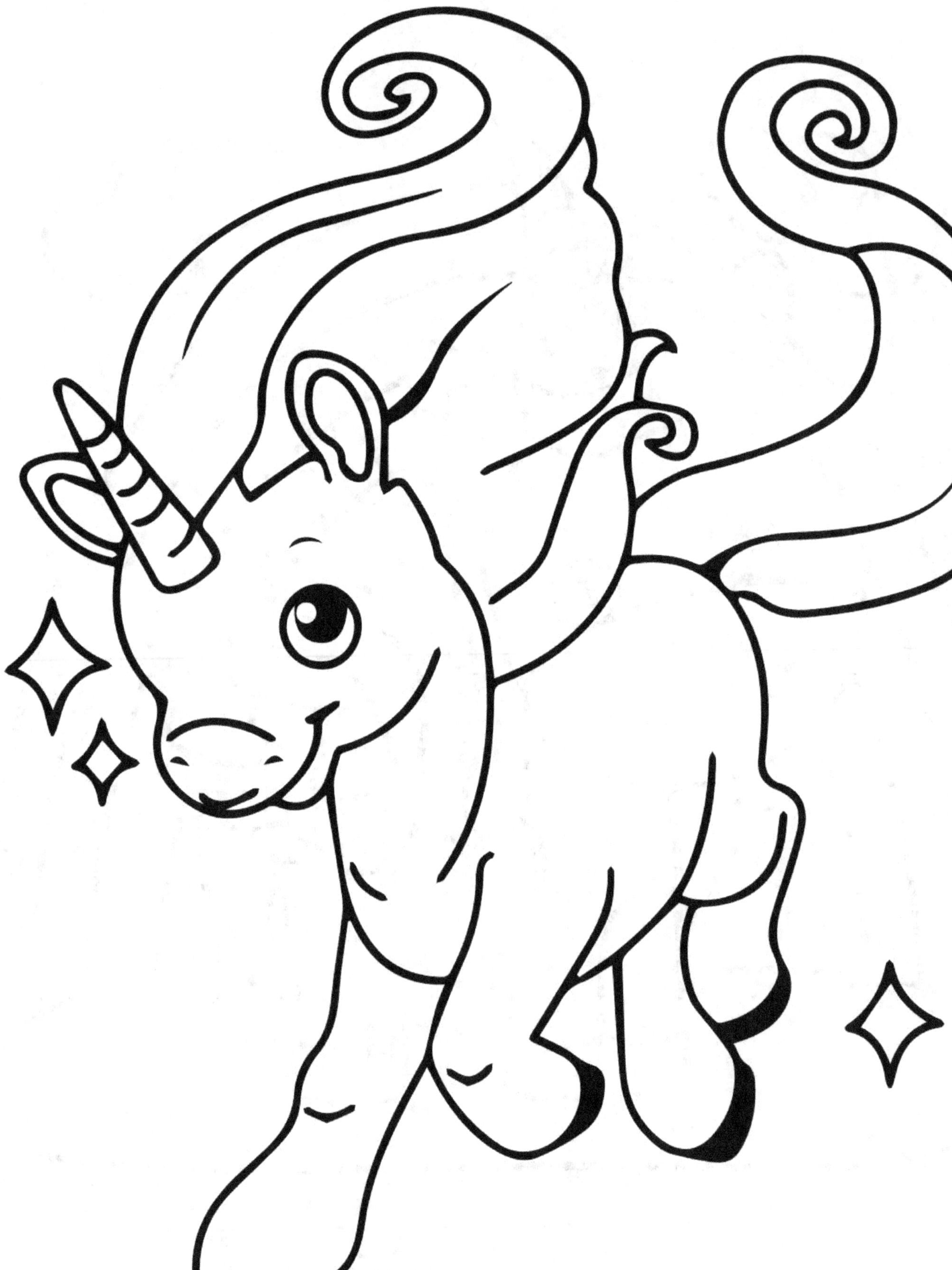

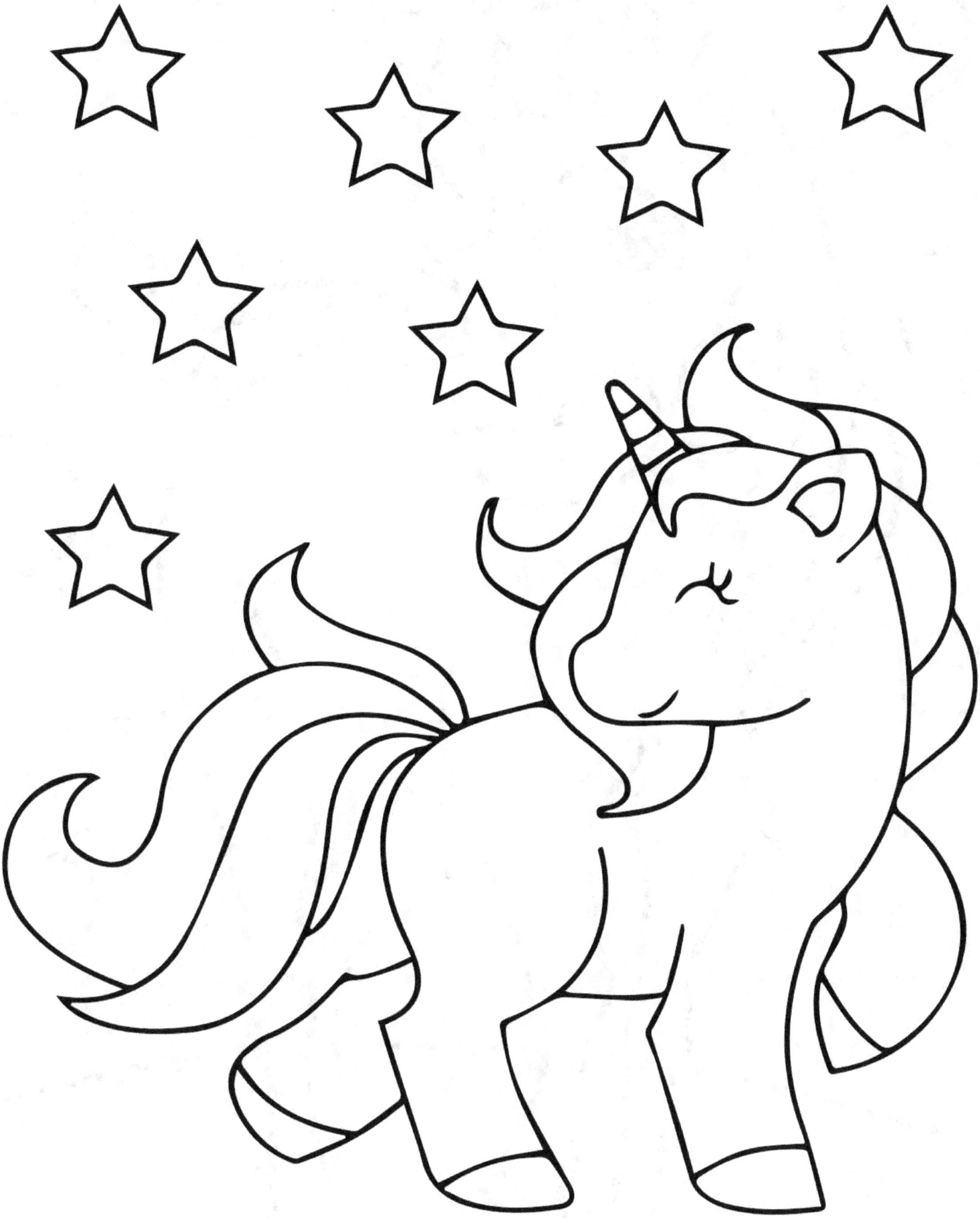

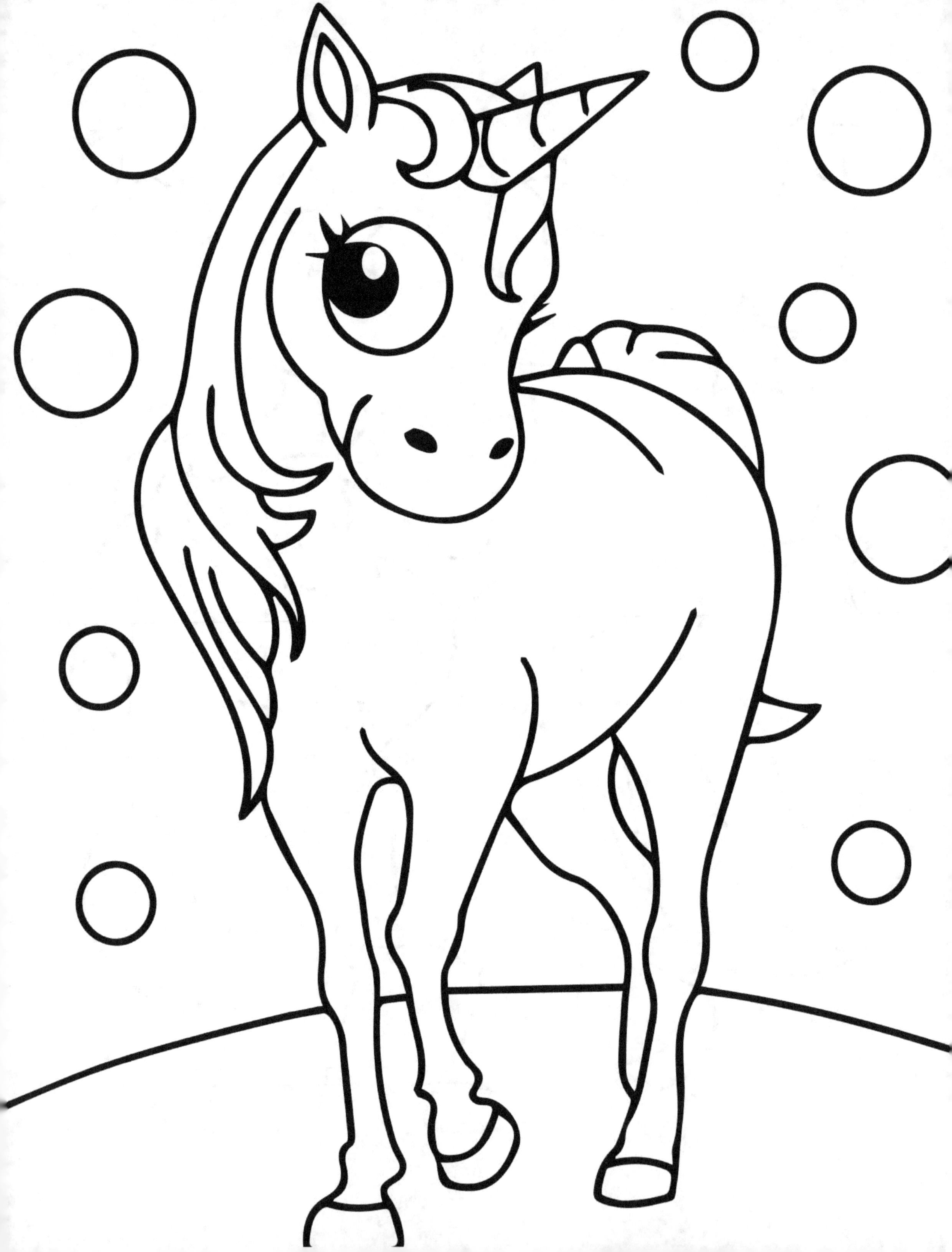

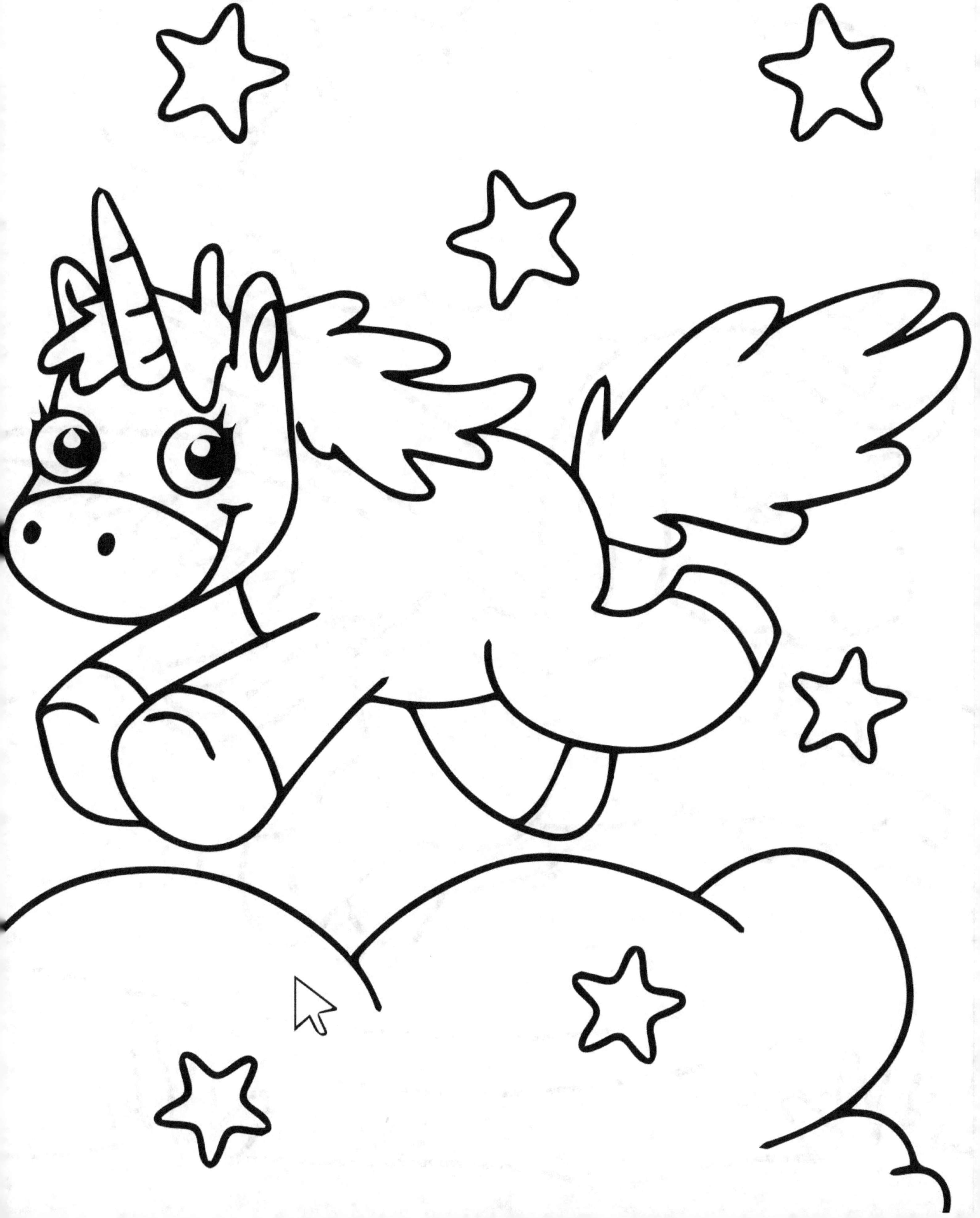

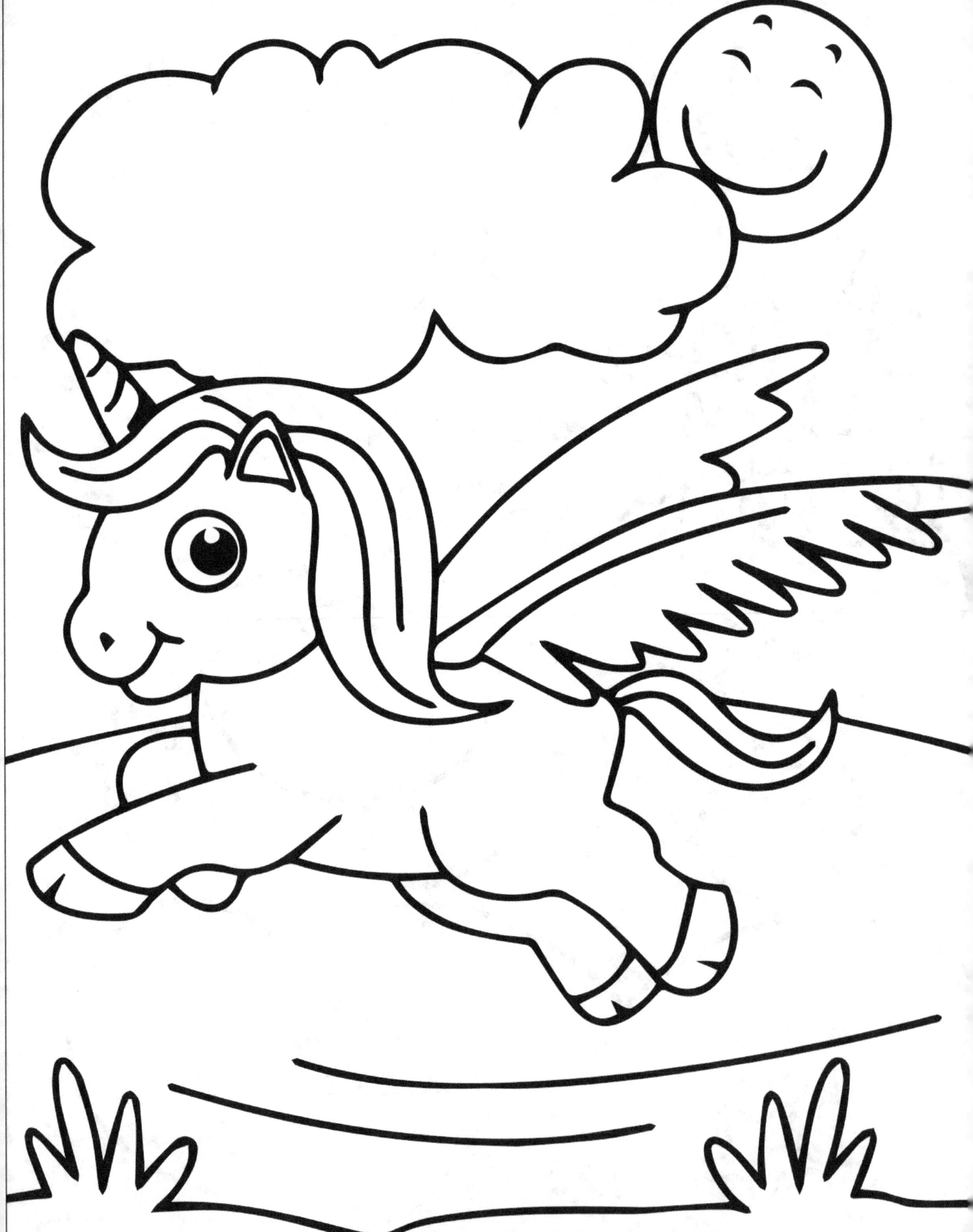

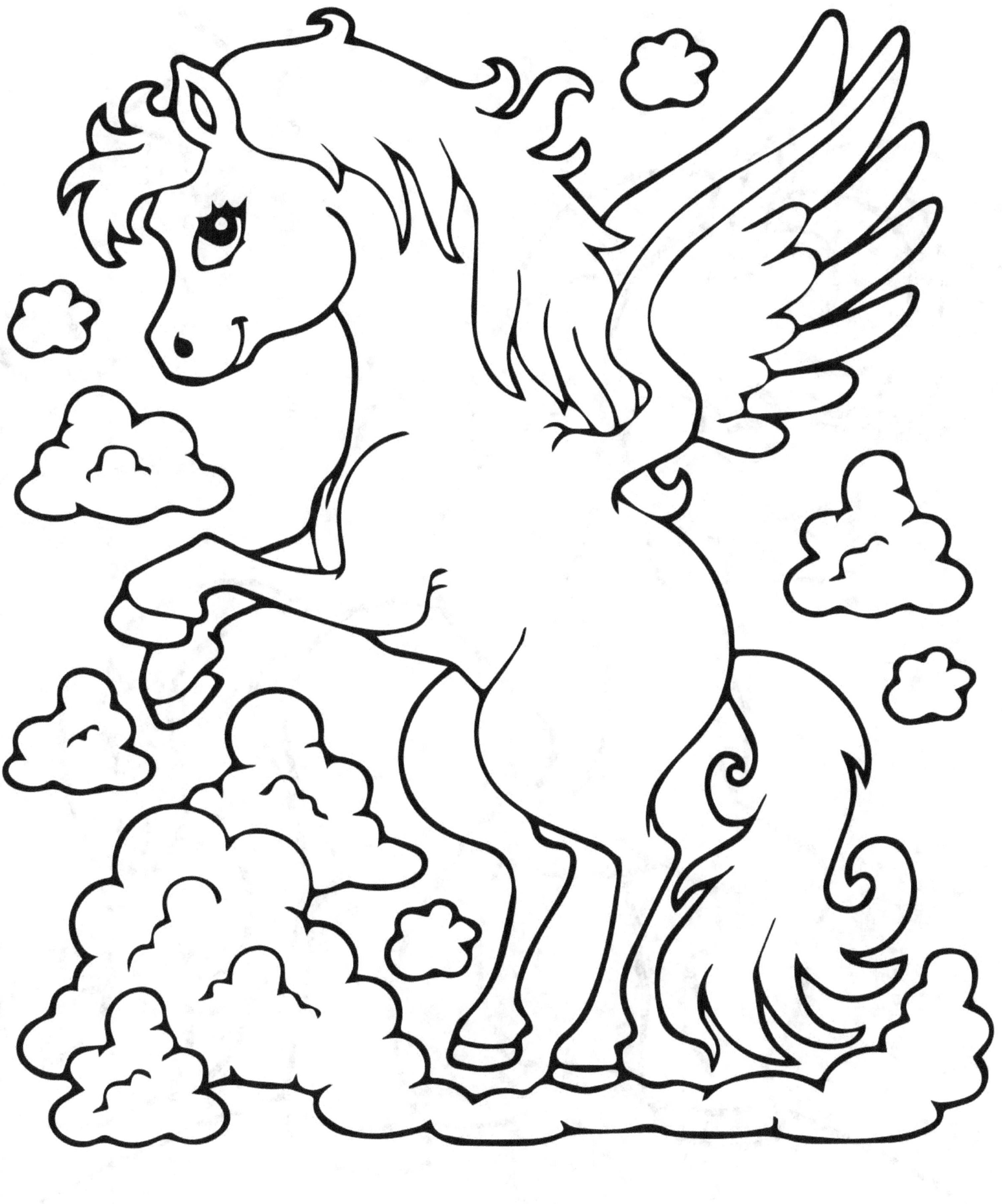

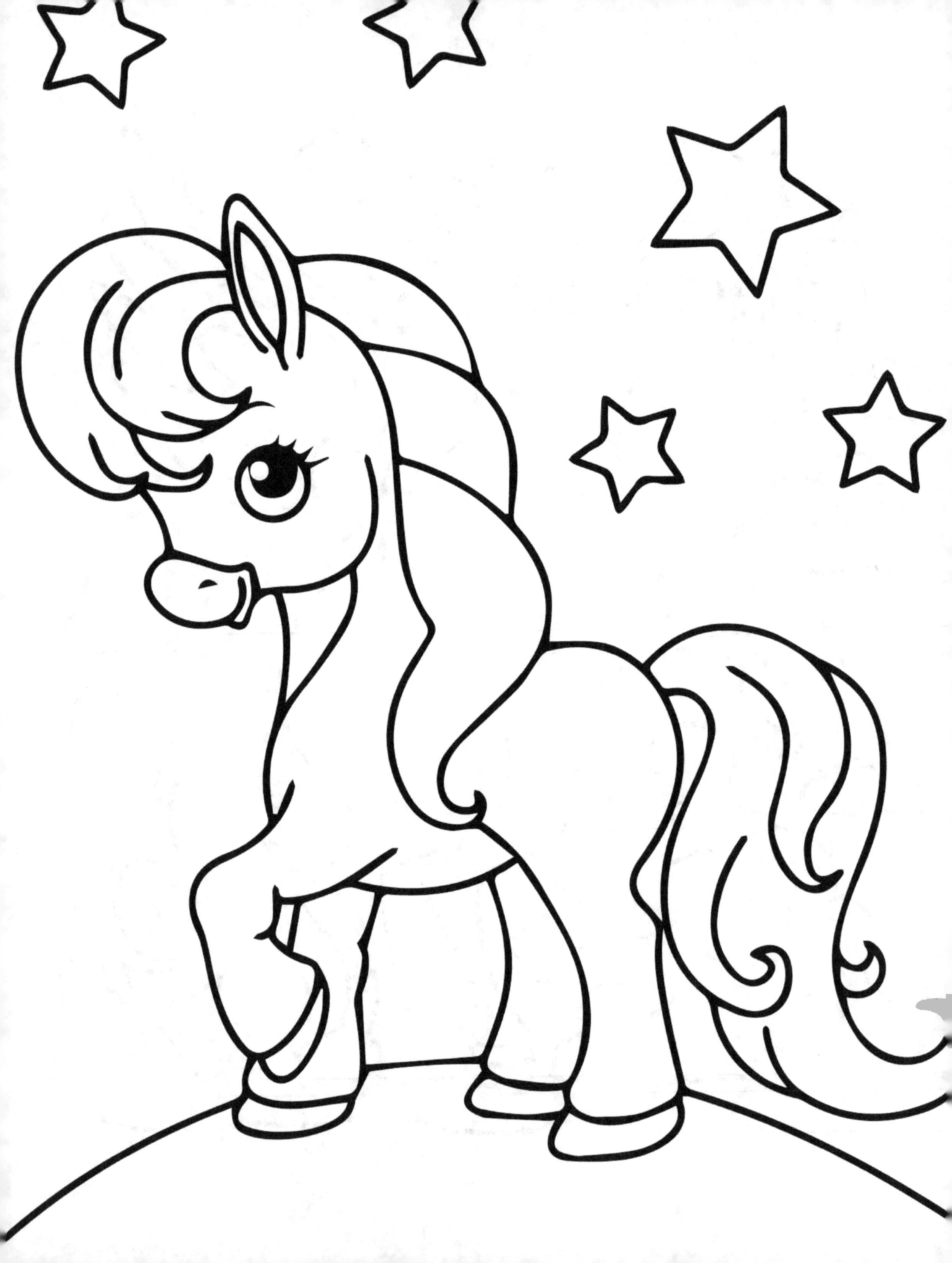

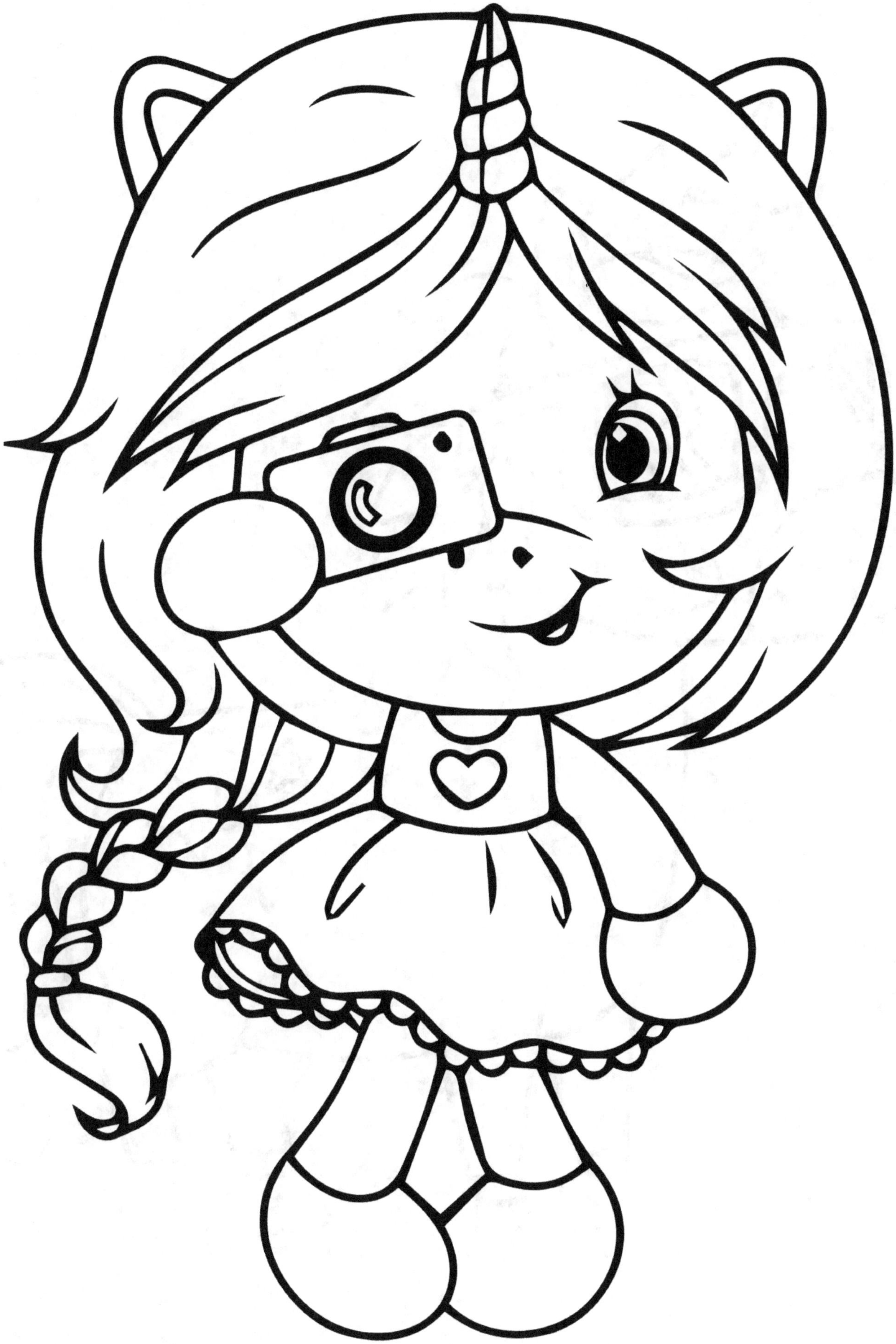

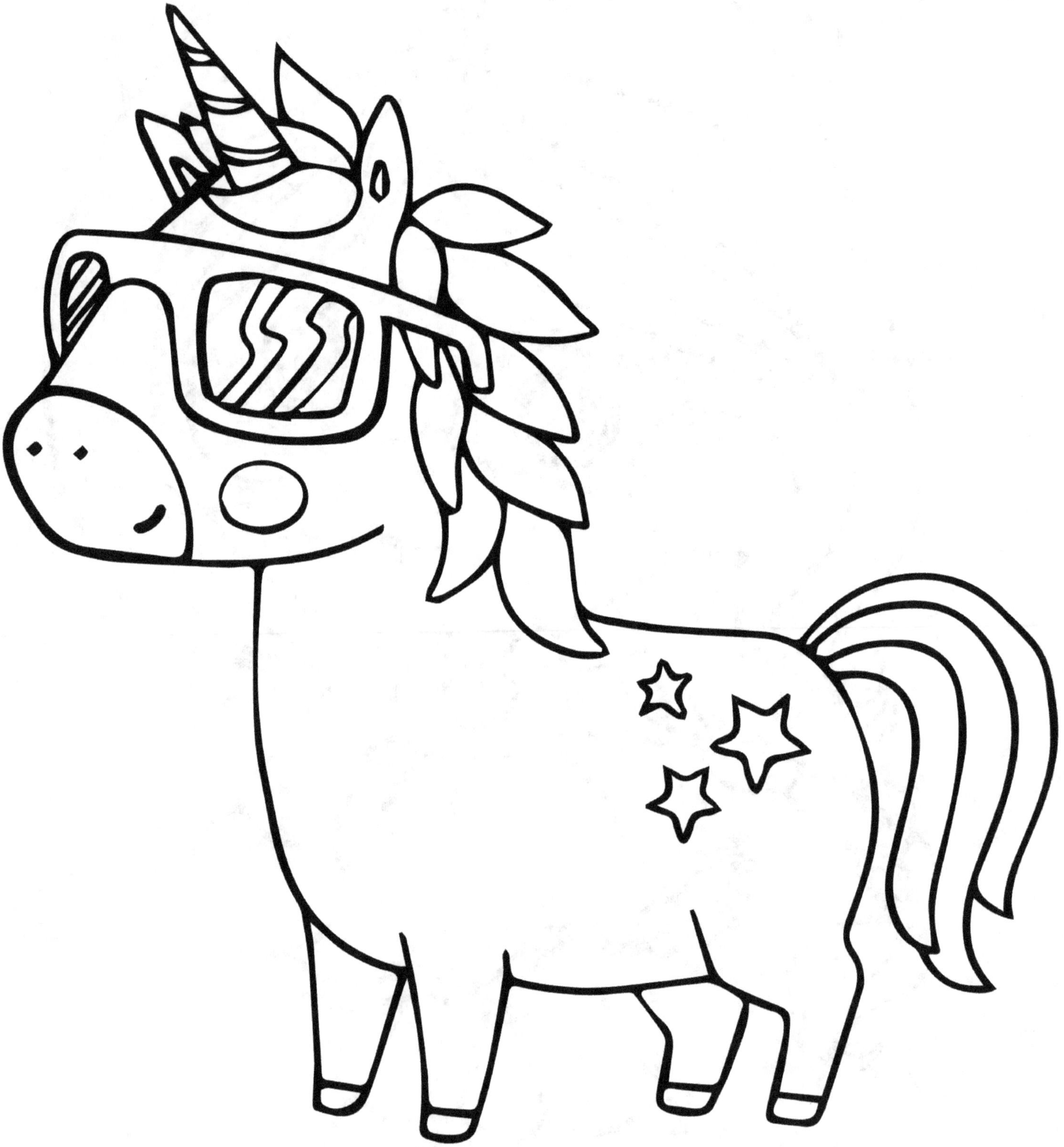

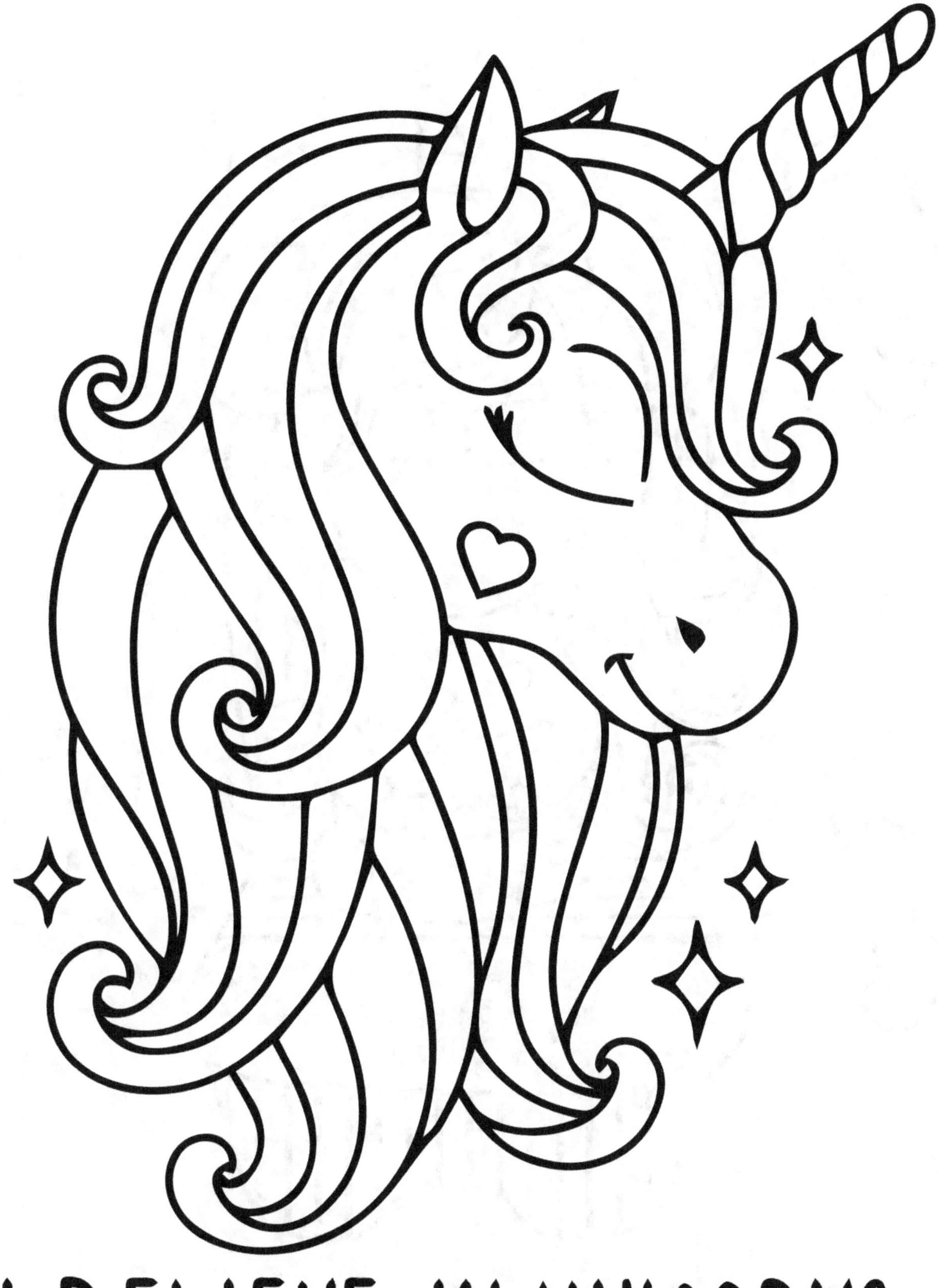

I BELIEVE IN UNICORNS

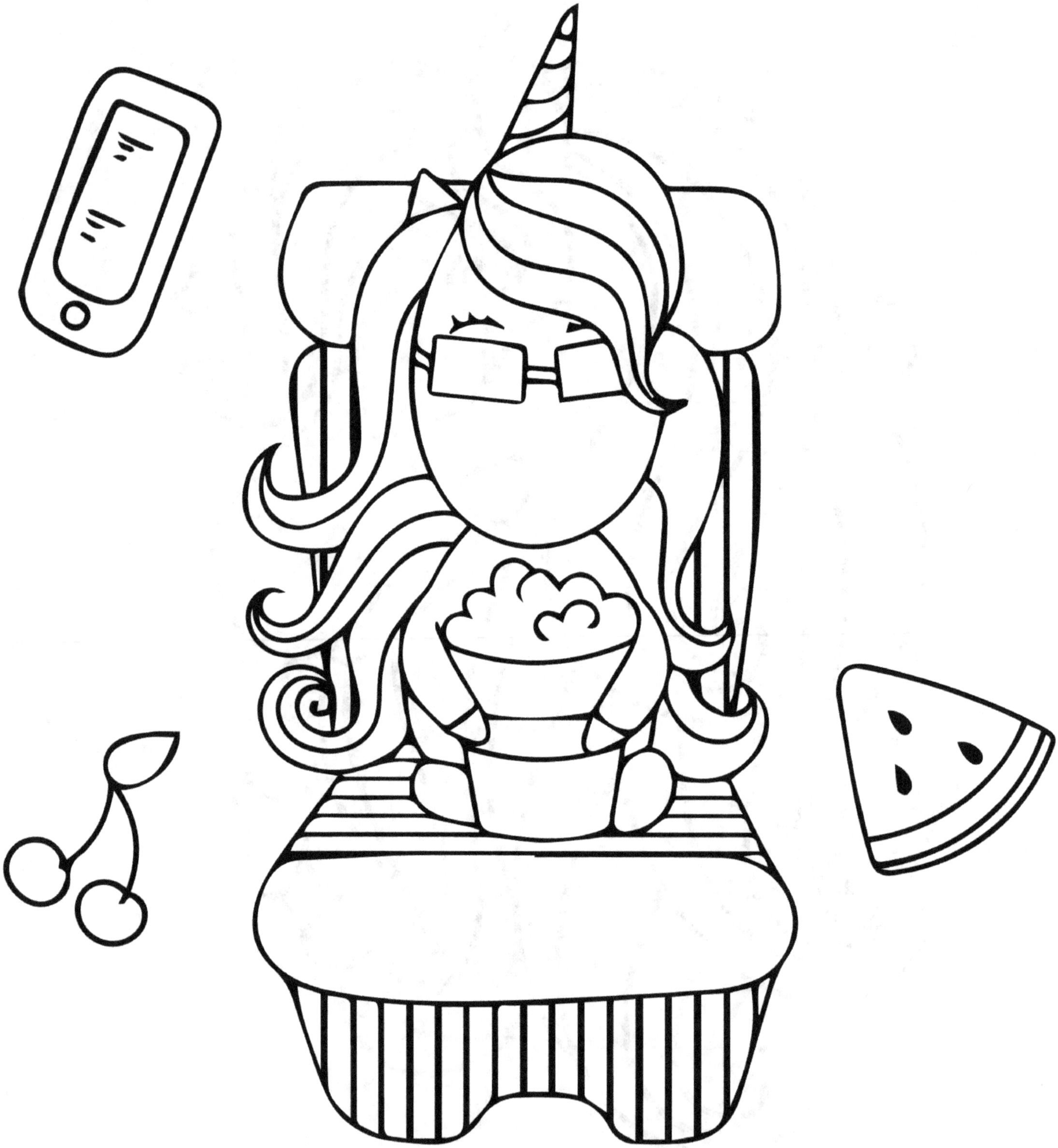

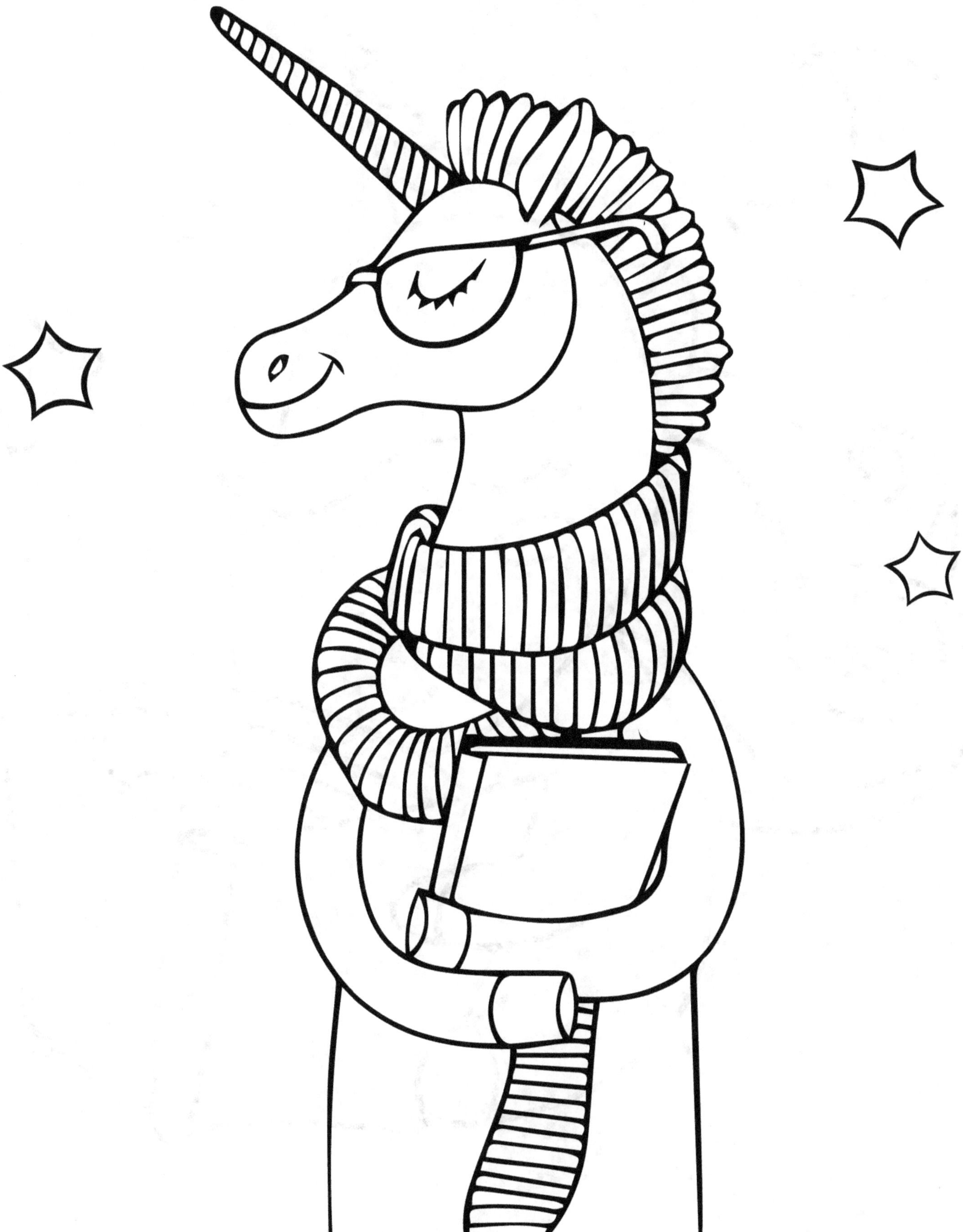

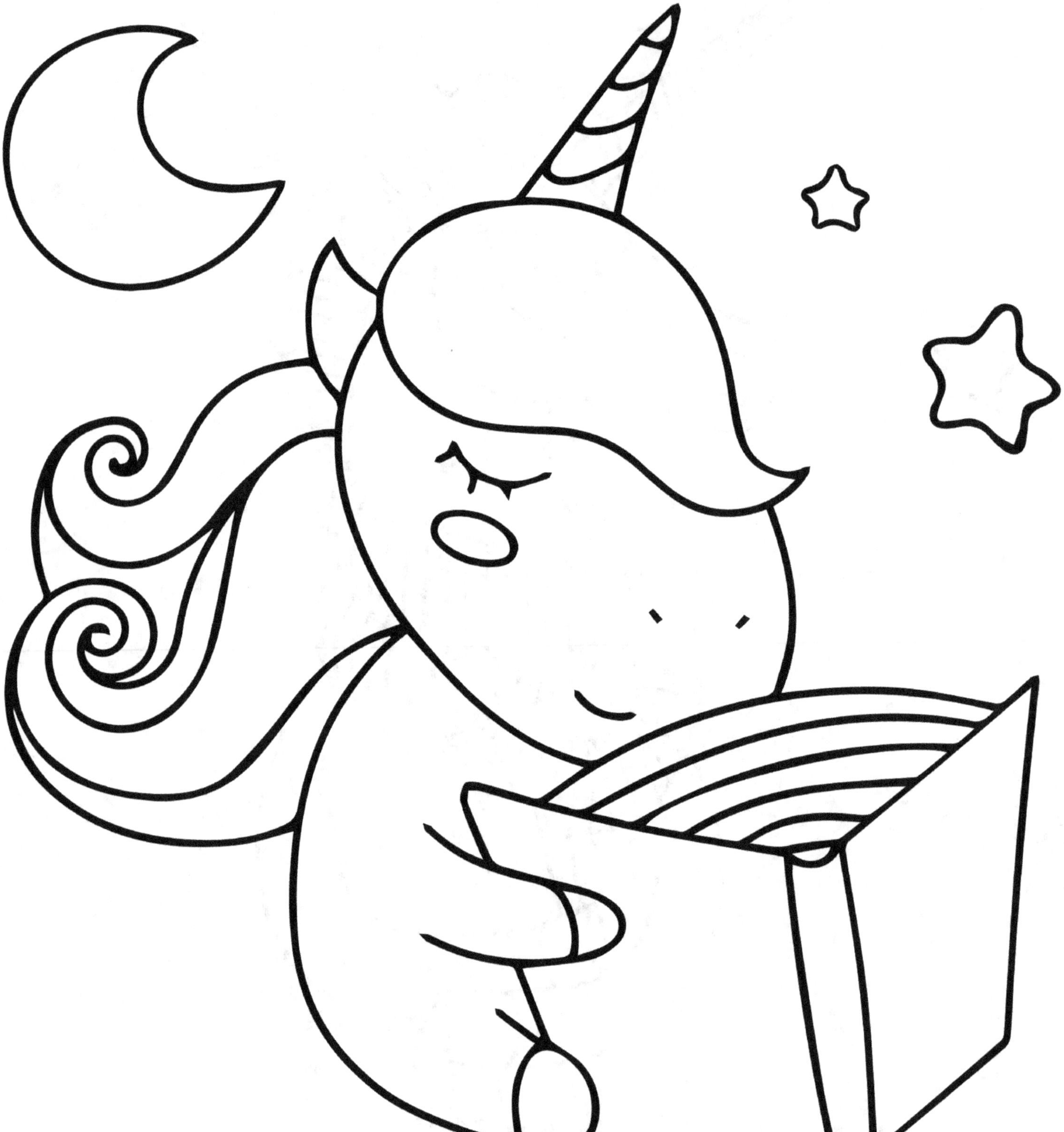

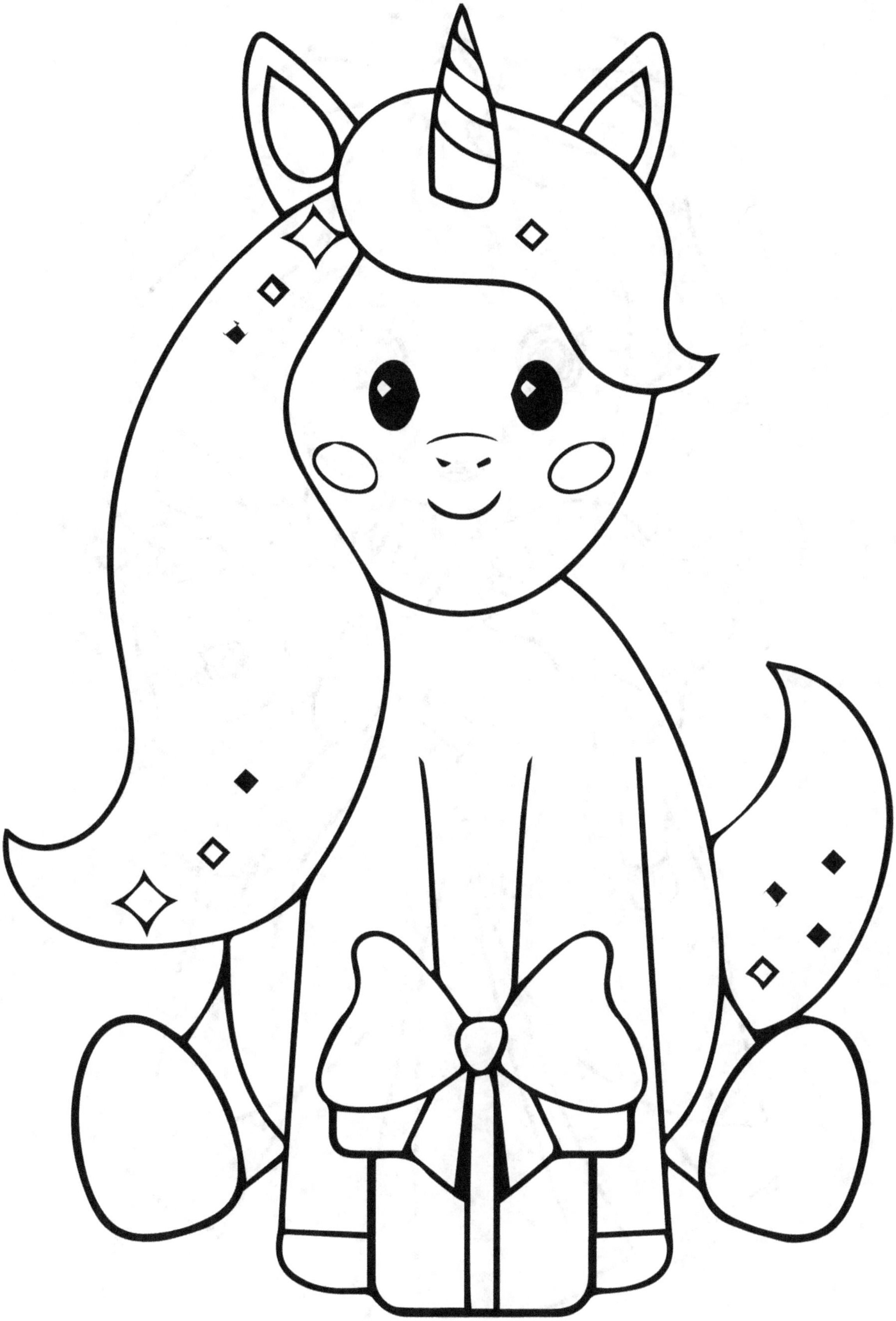

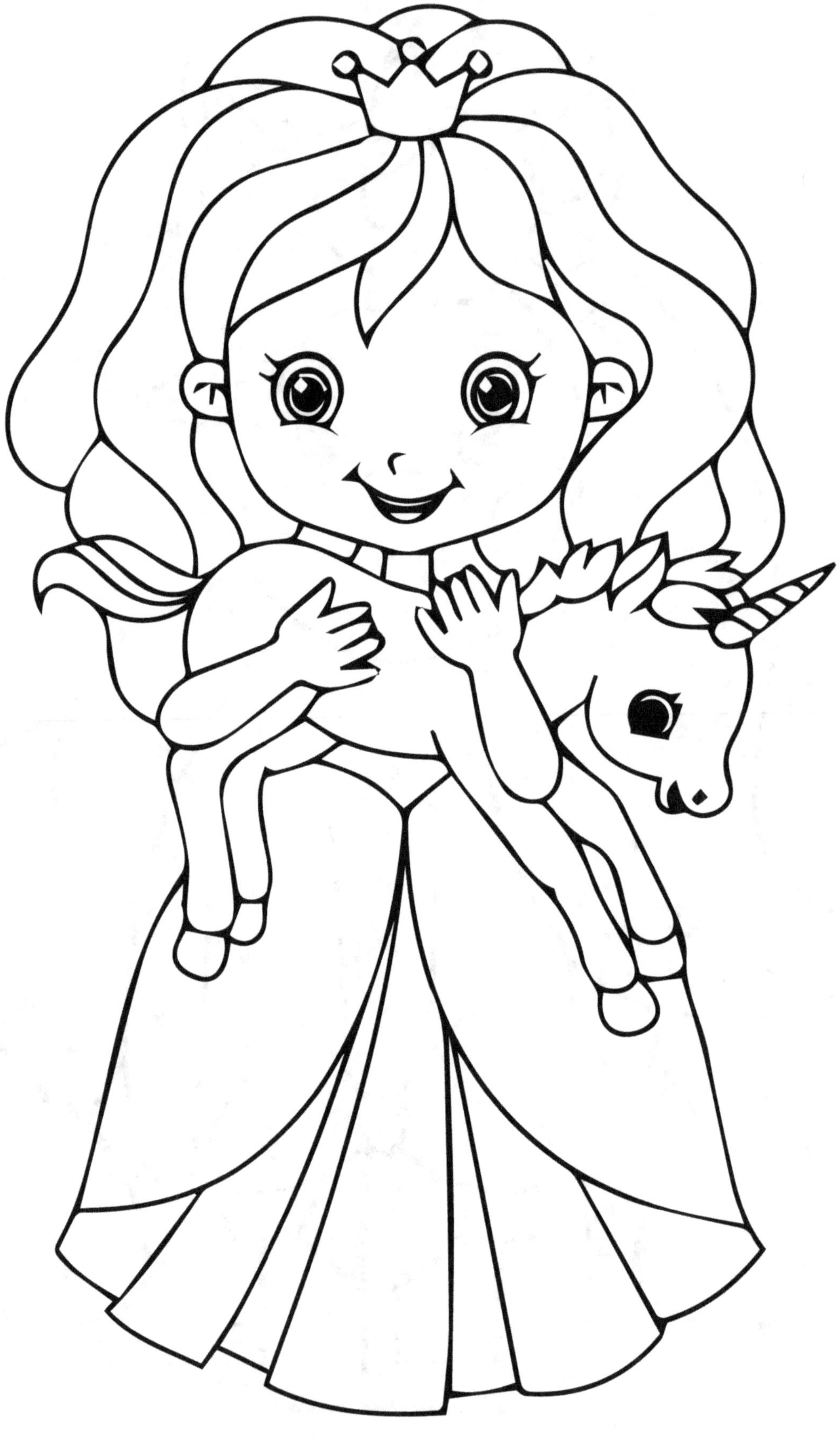

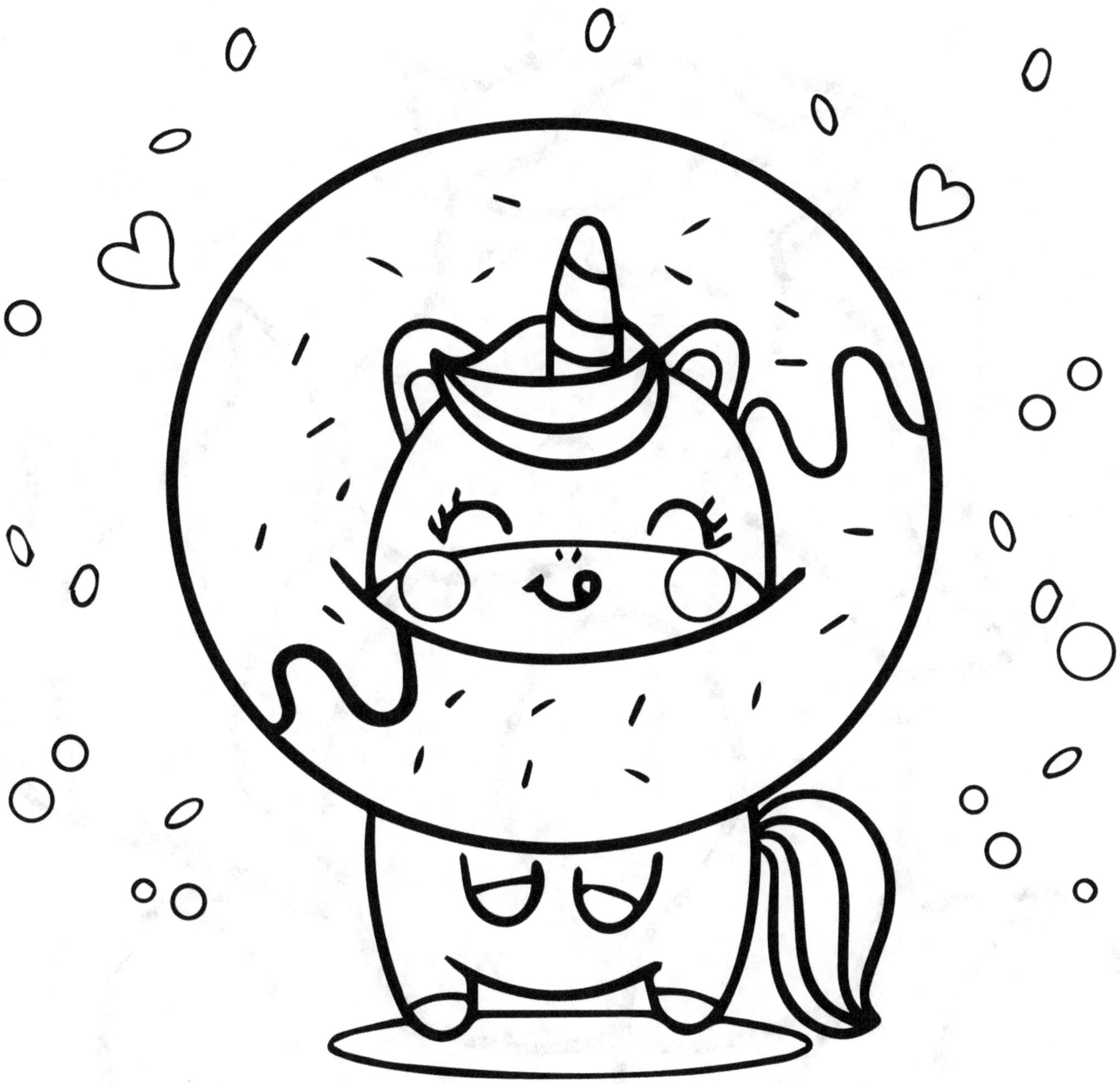

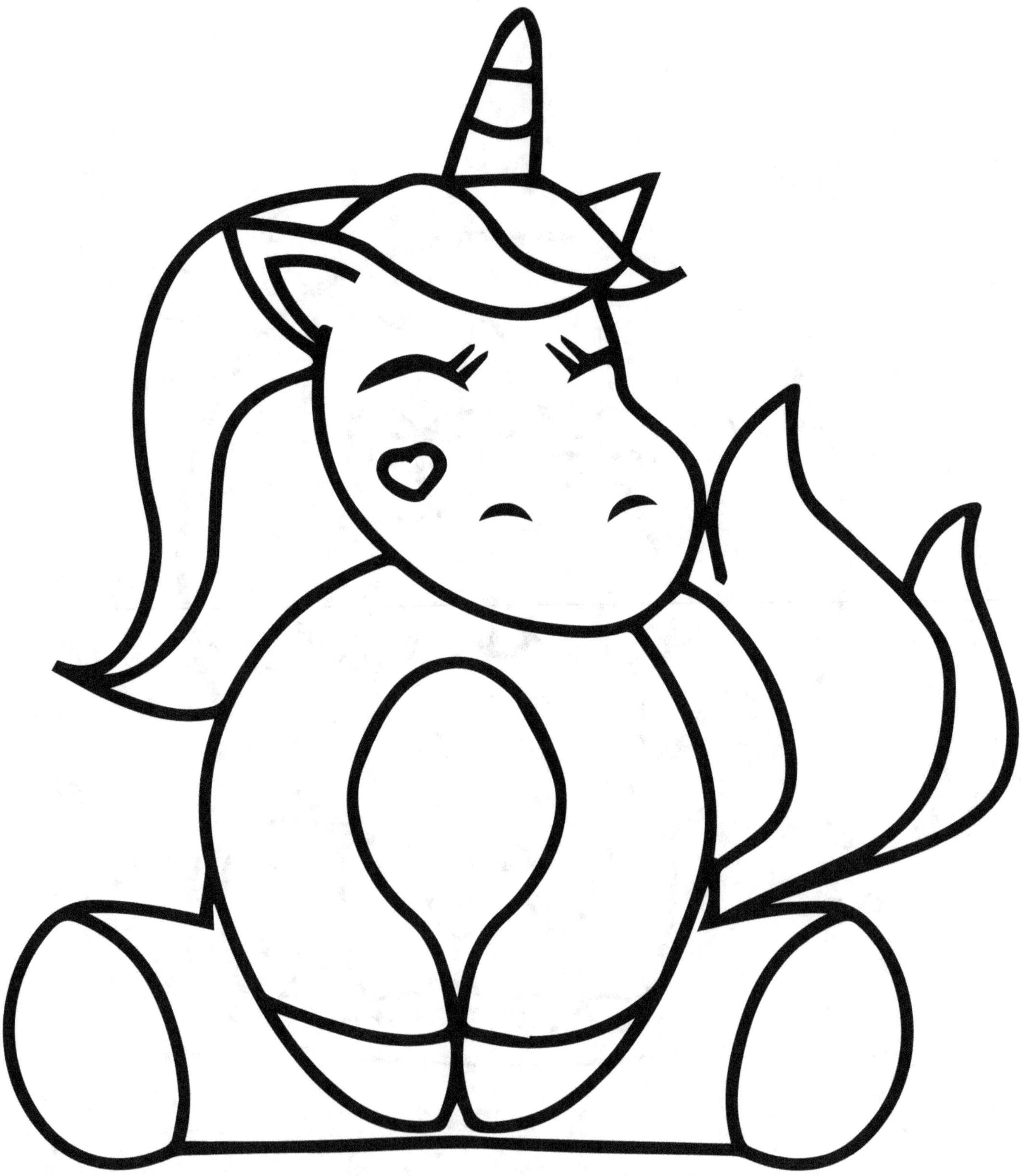

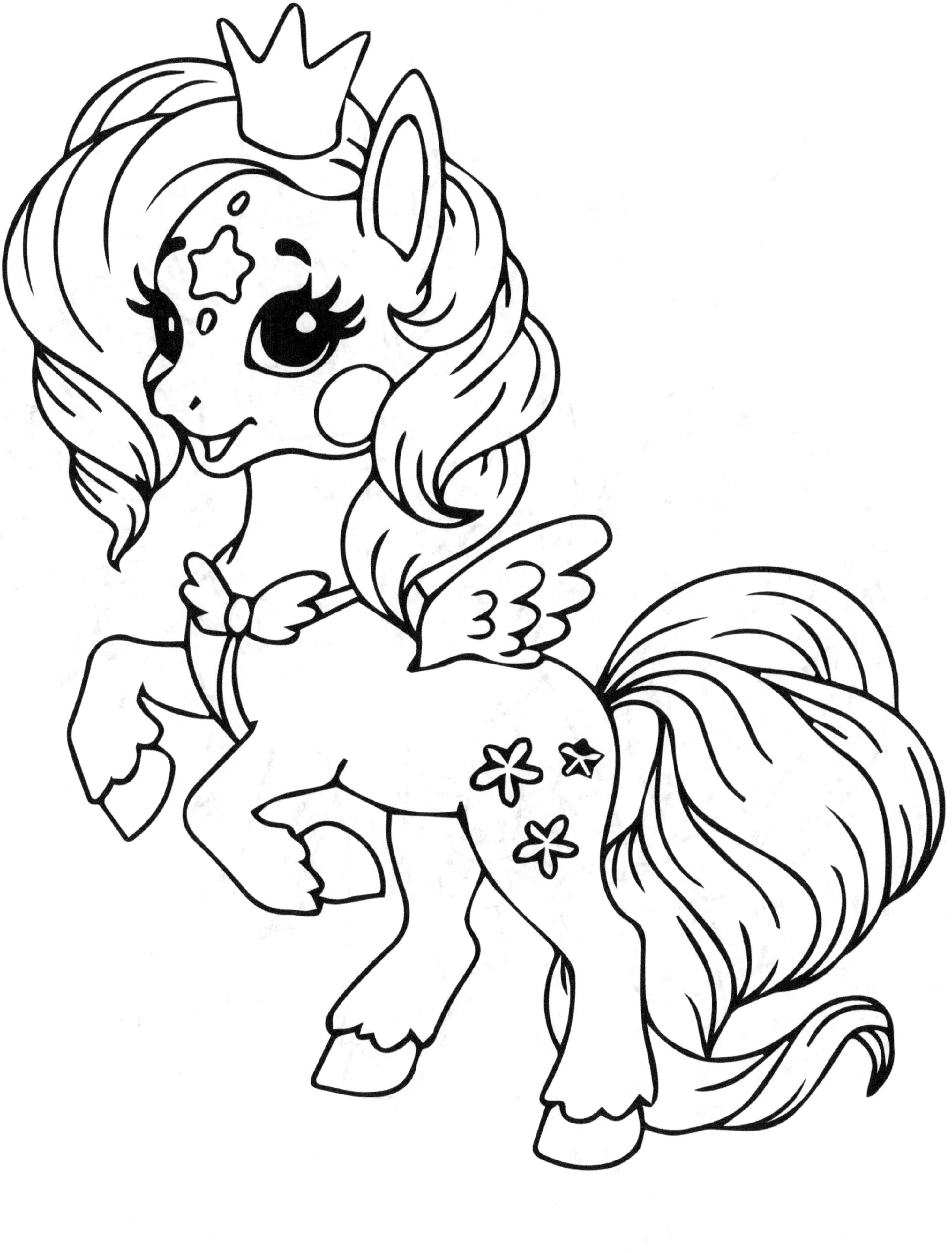

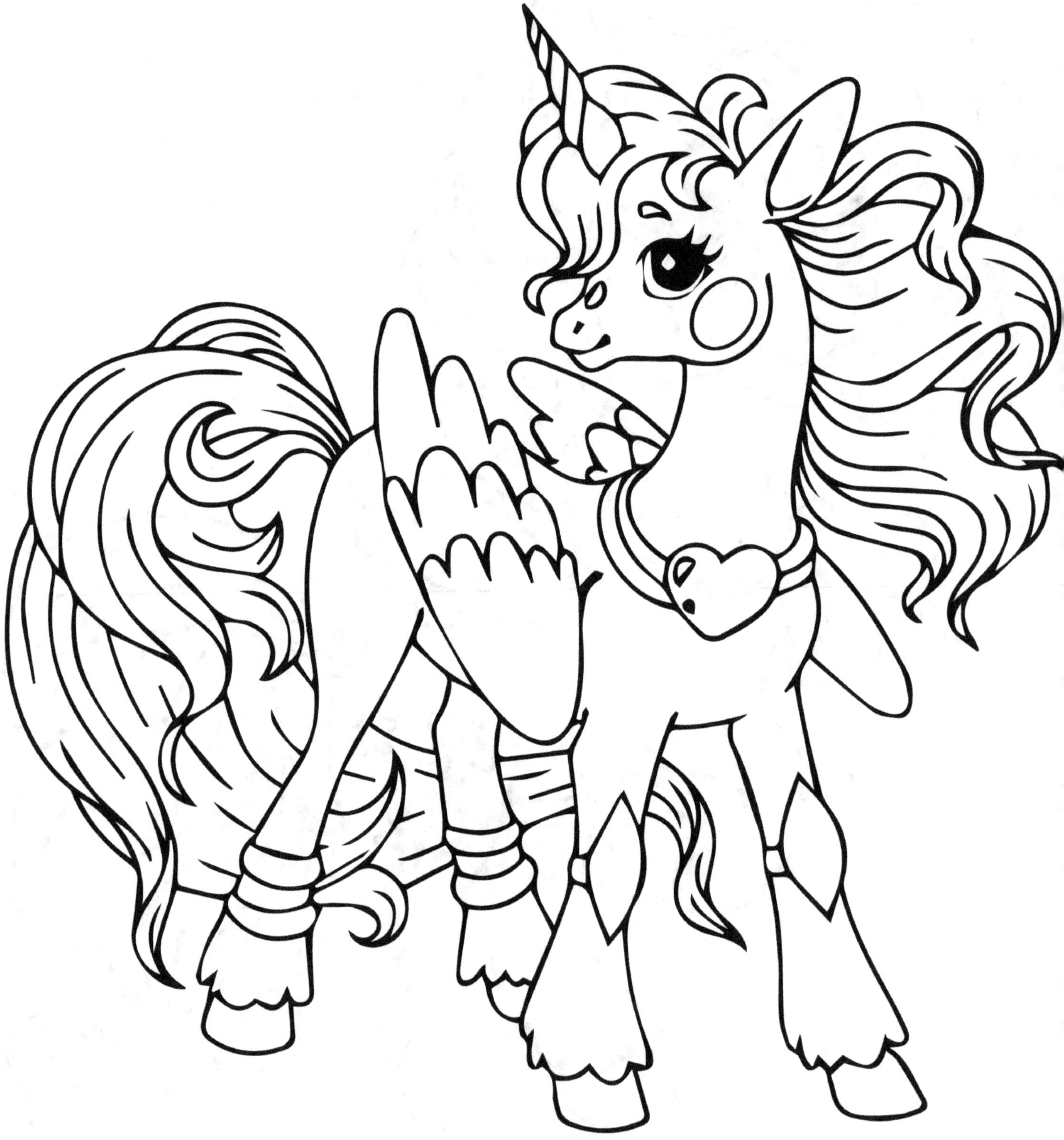

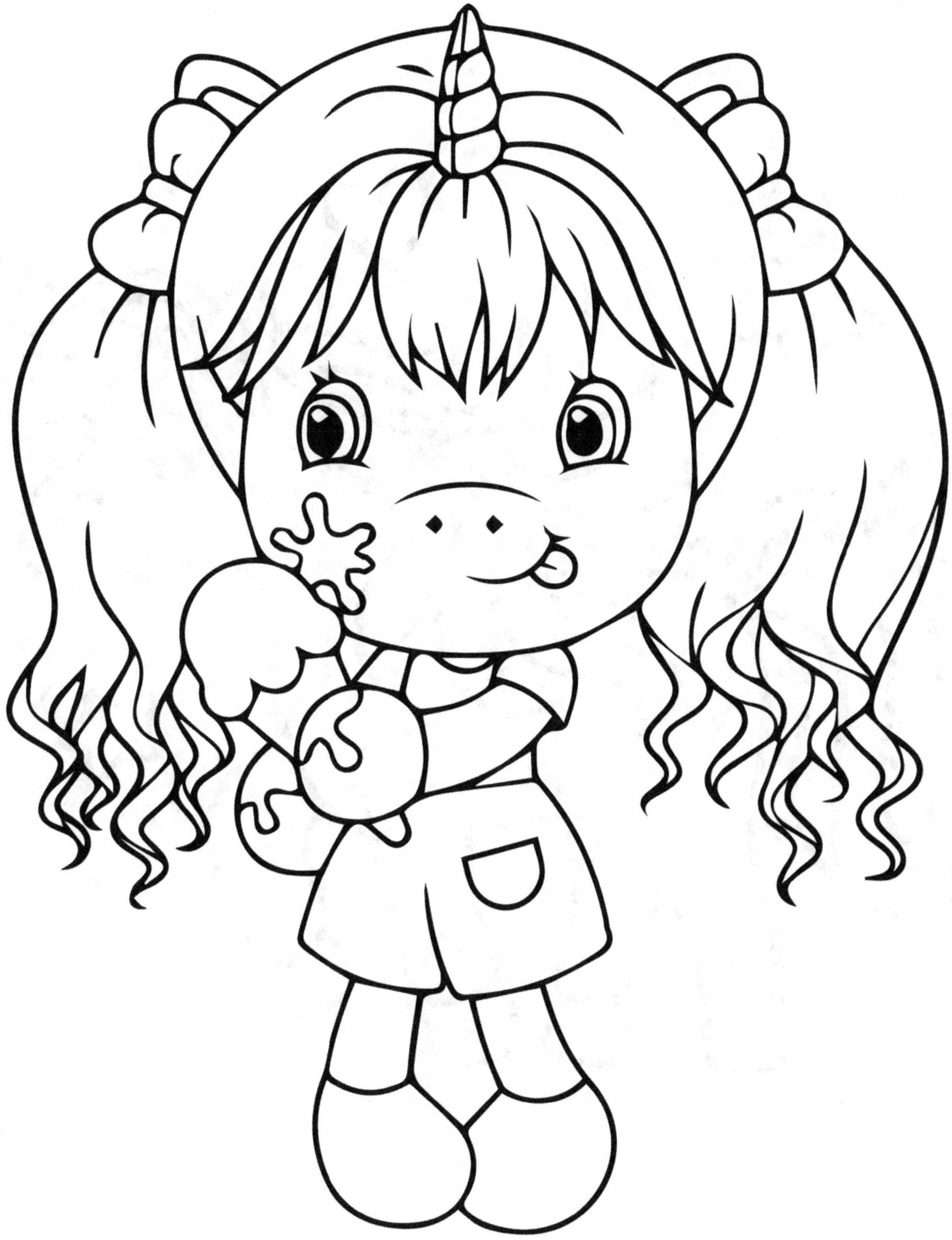

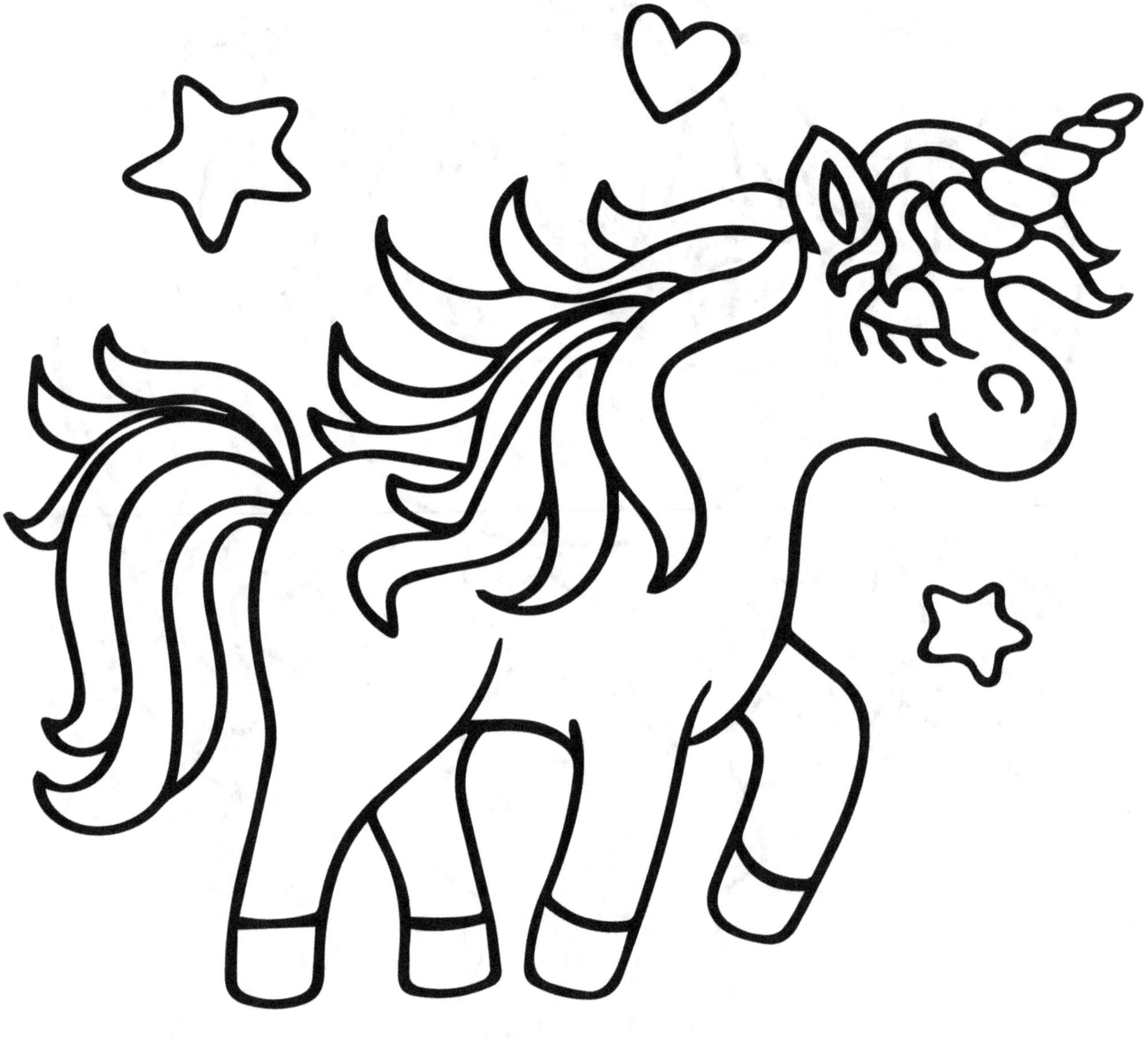

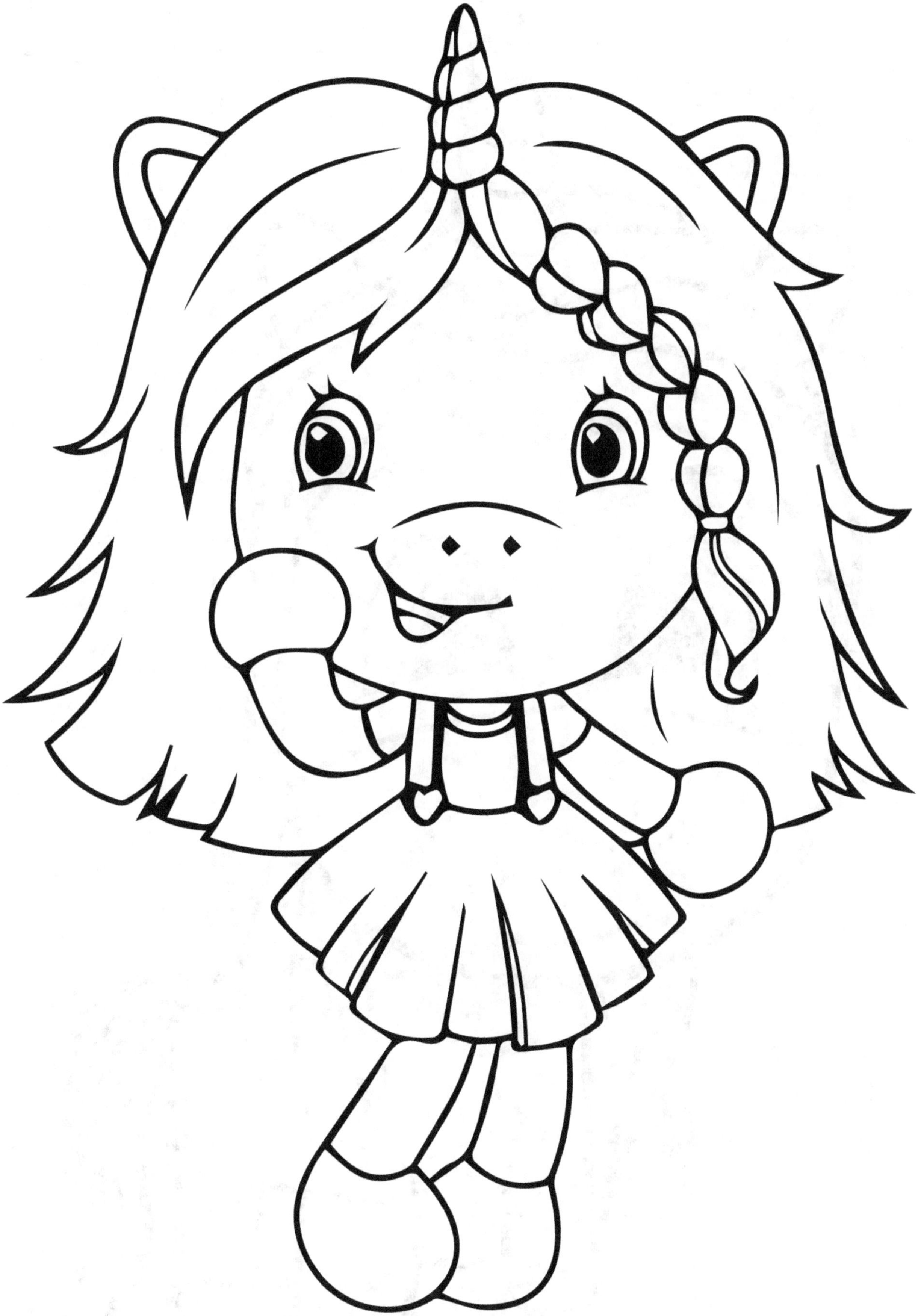

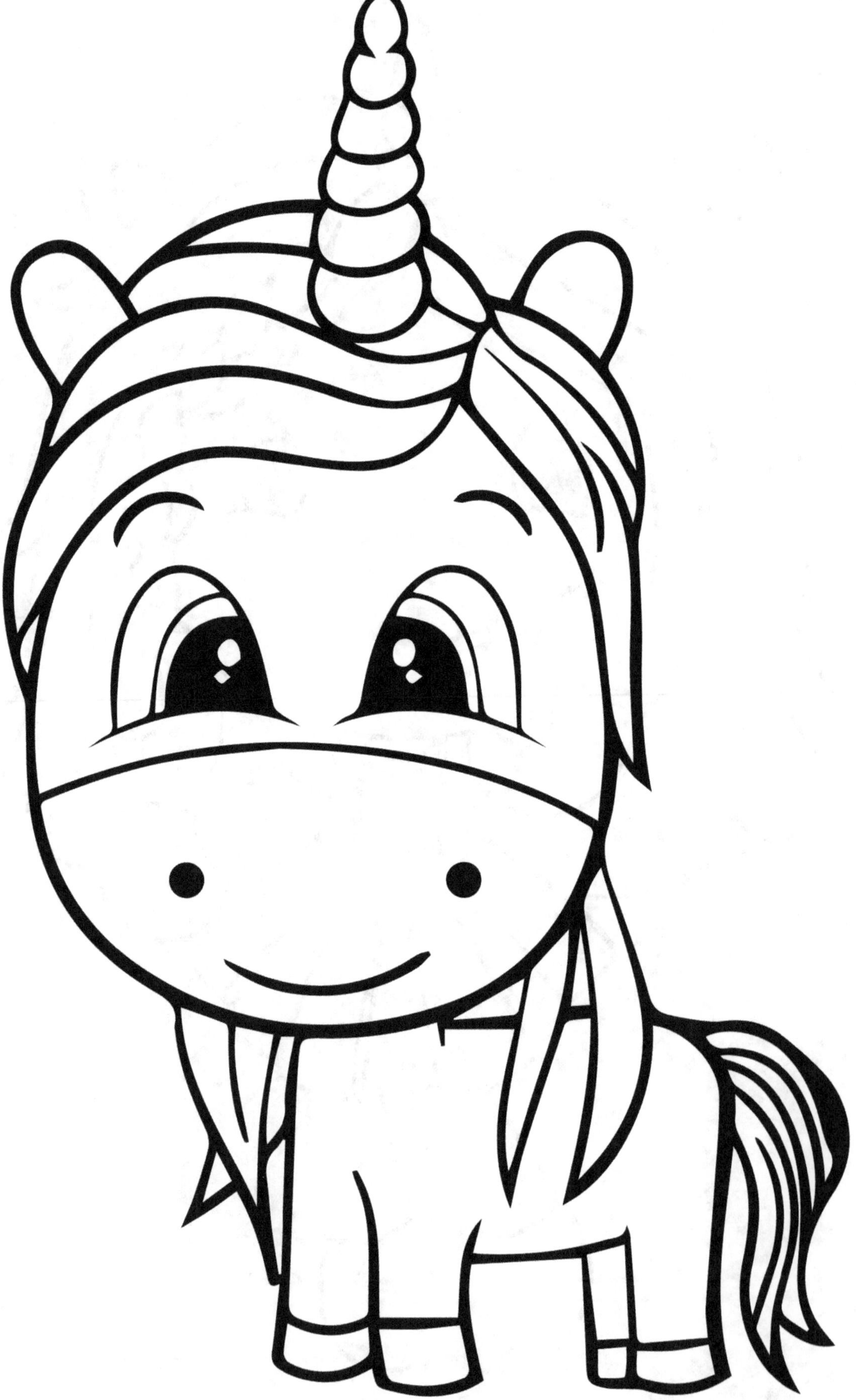

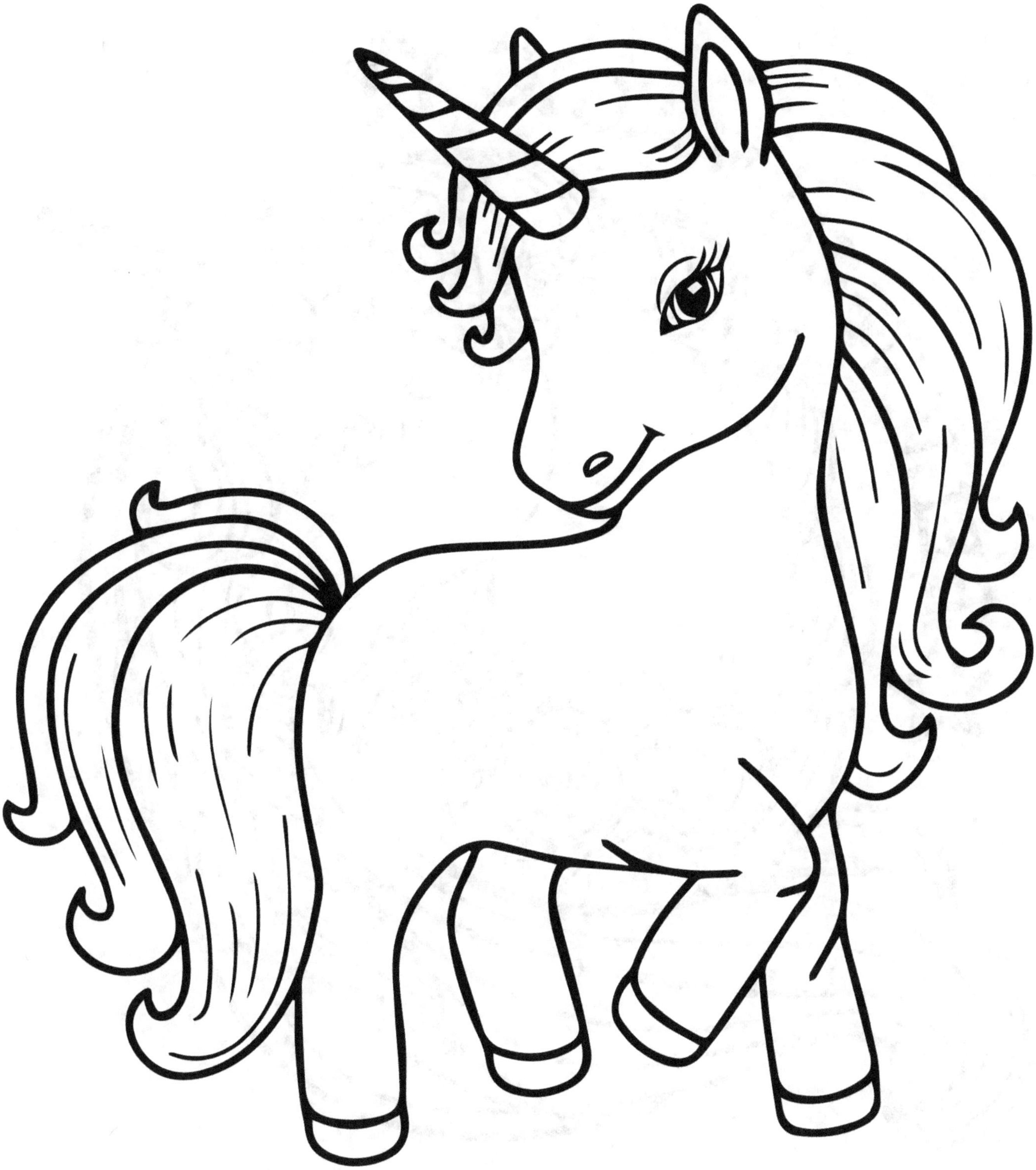

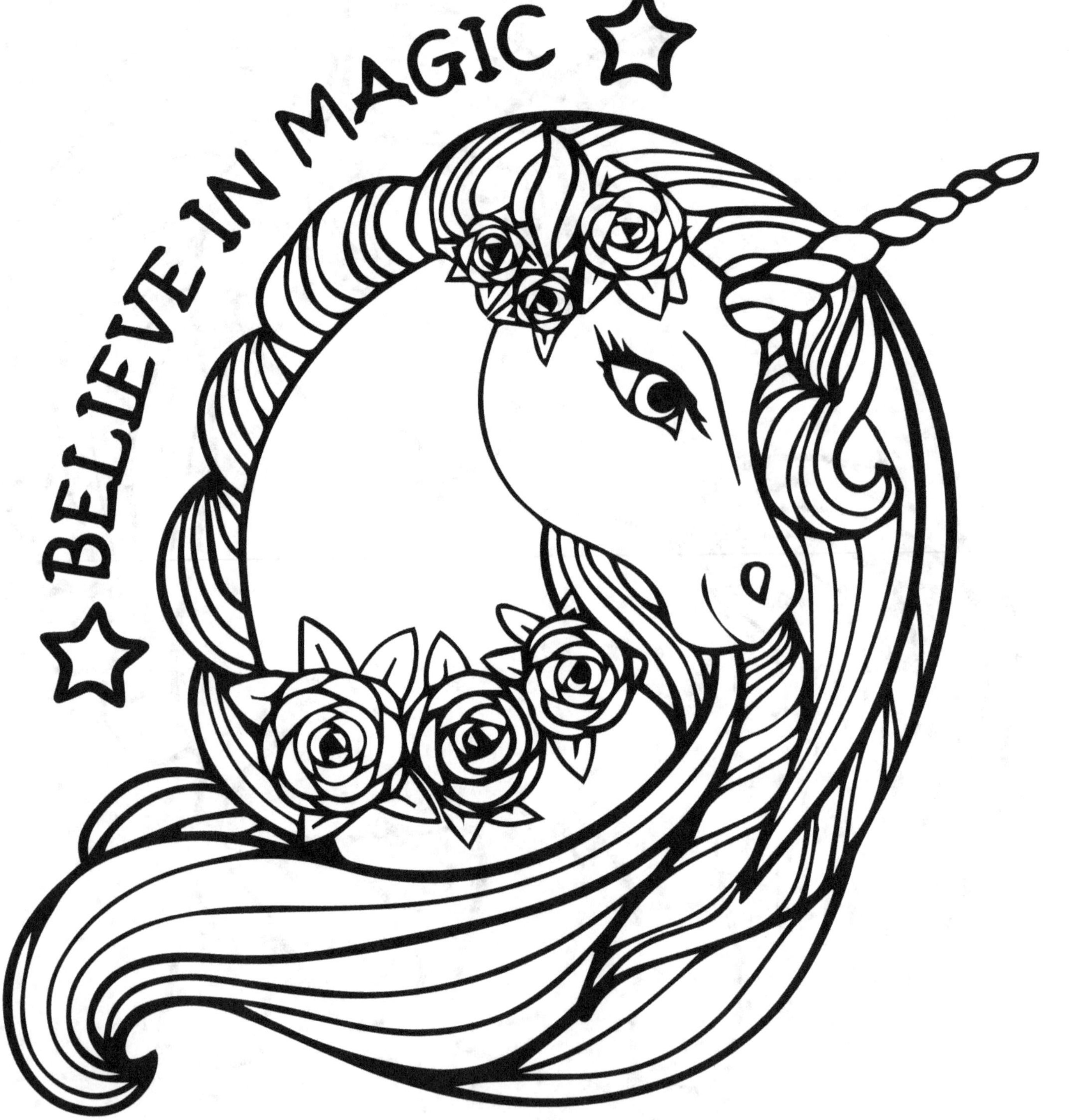
BELIEVE IN MAGIC

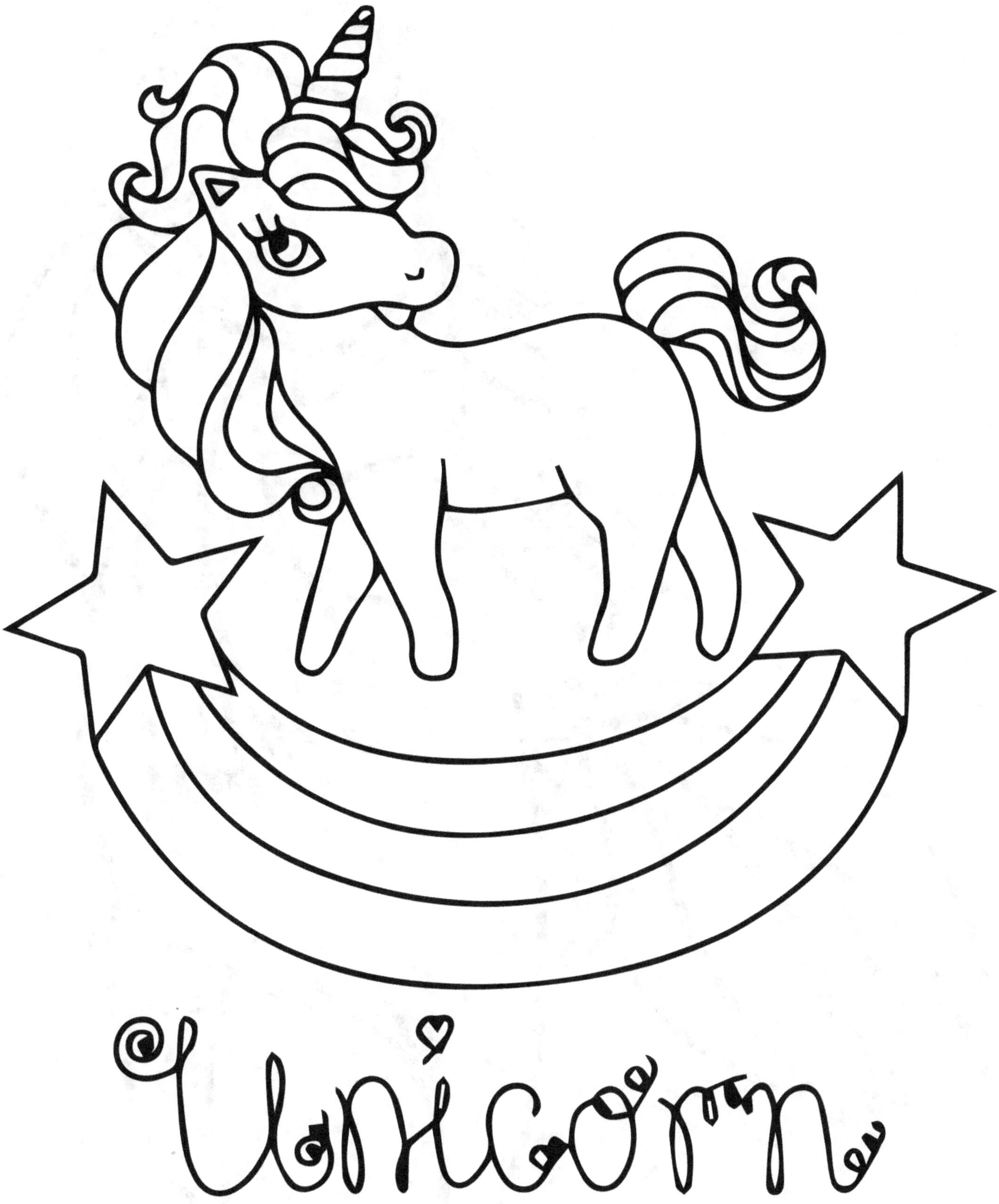
Unicorn

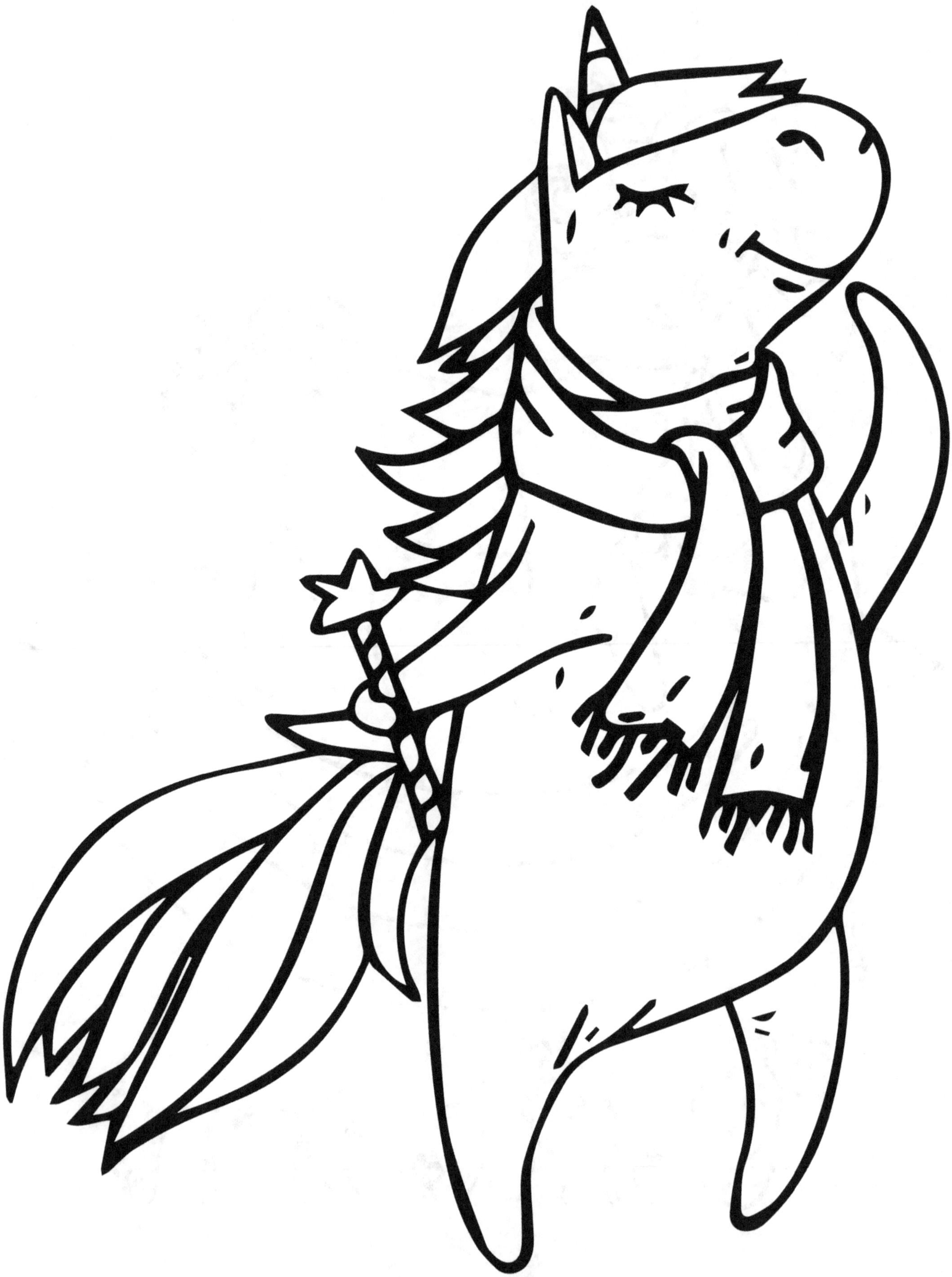

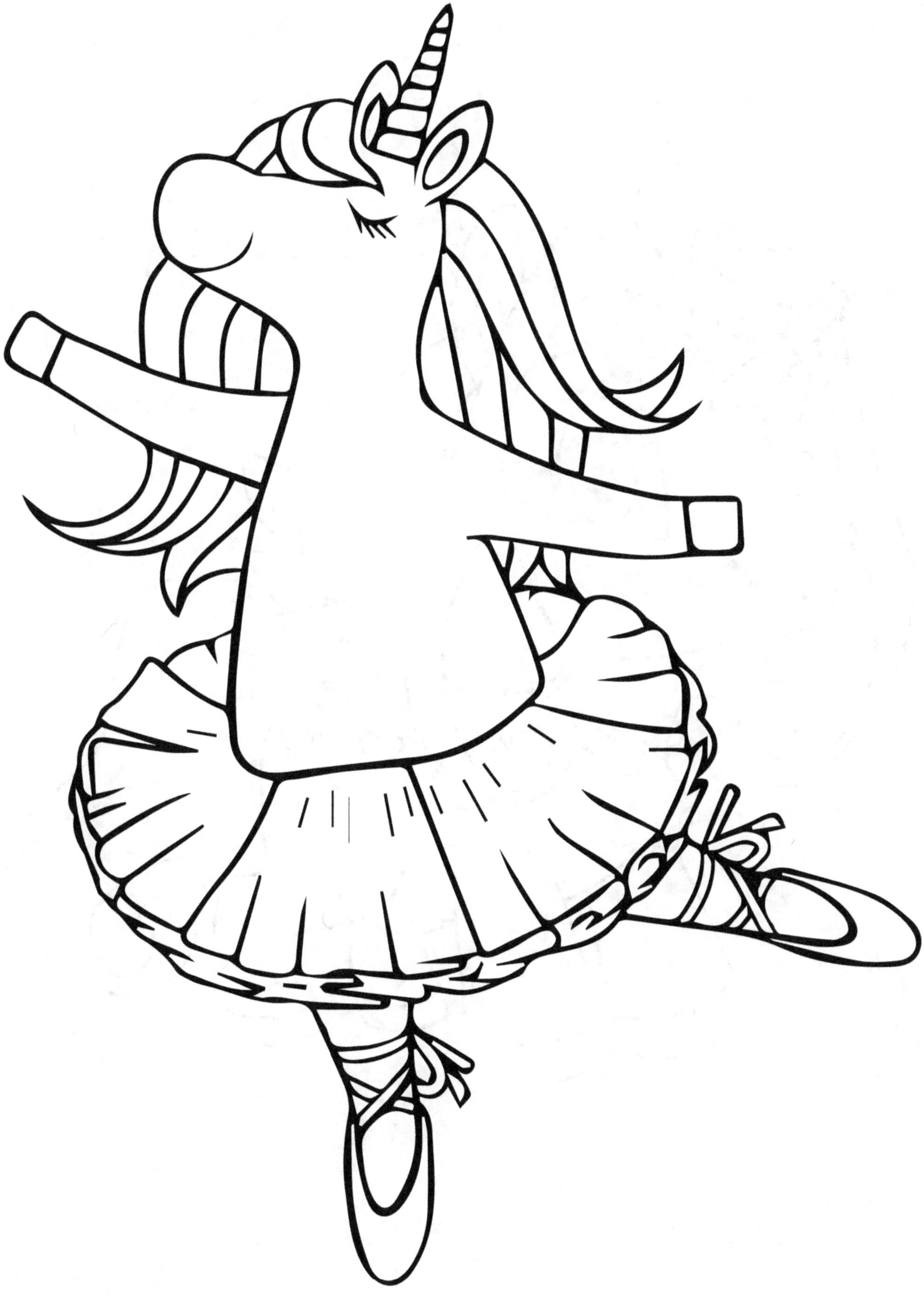

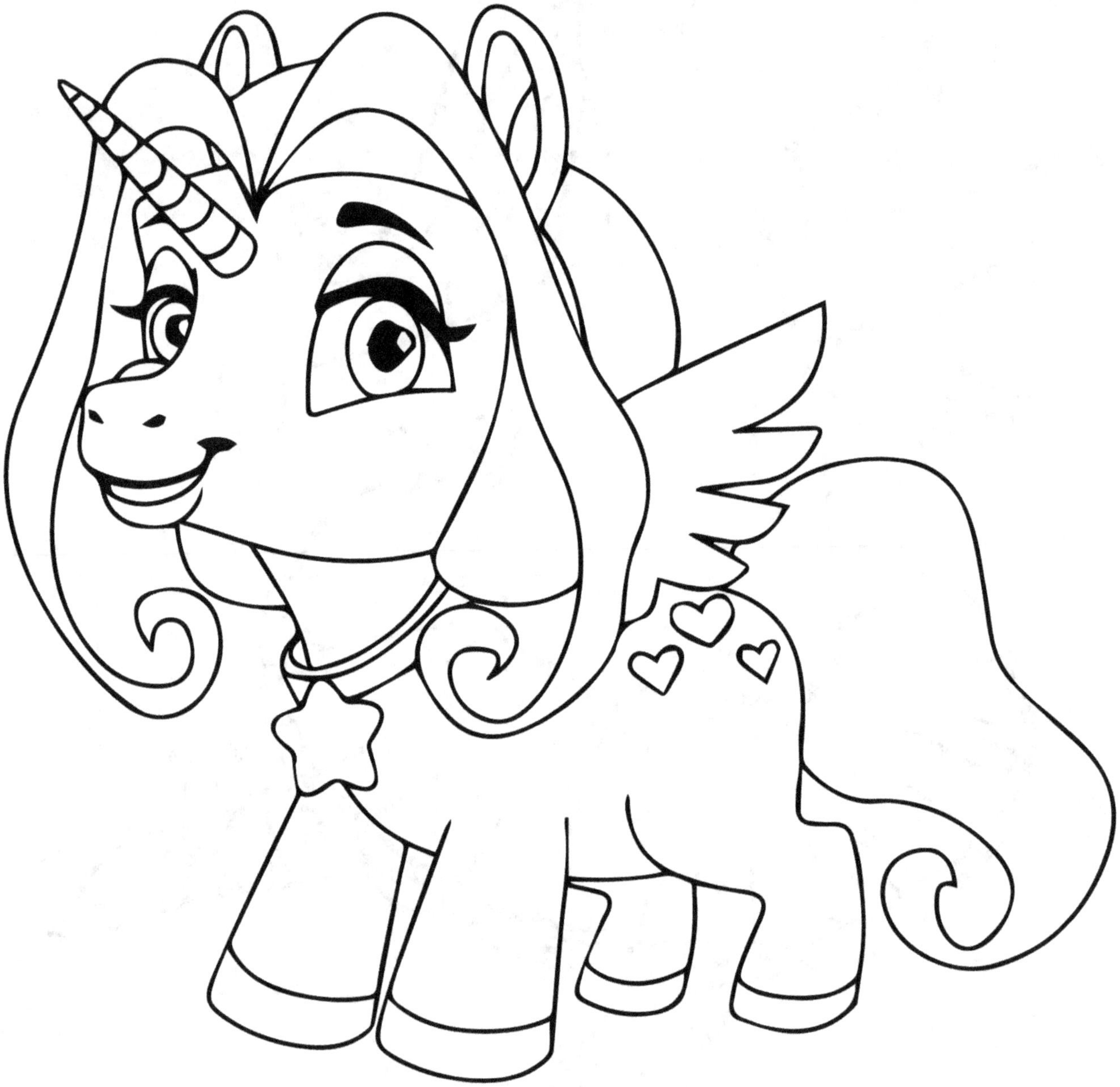

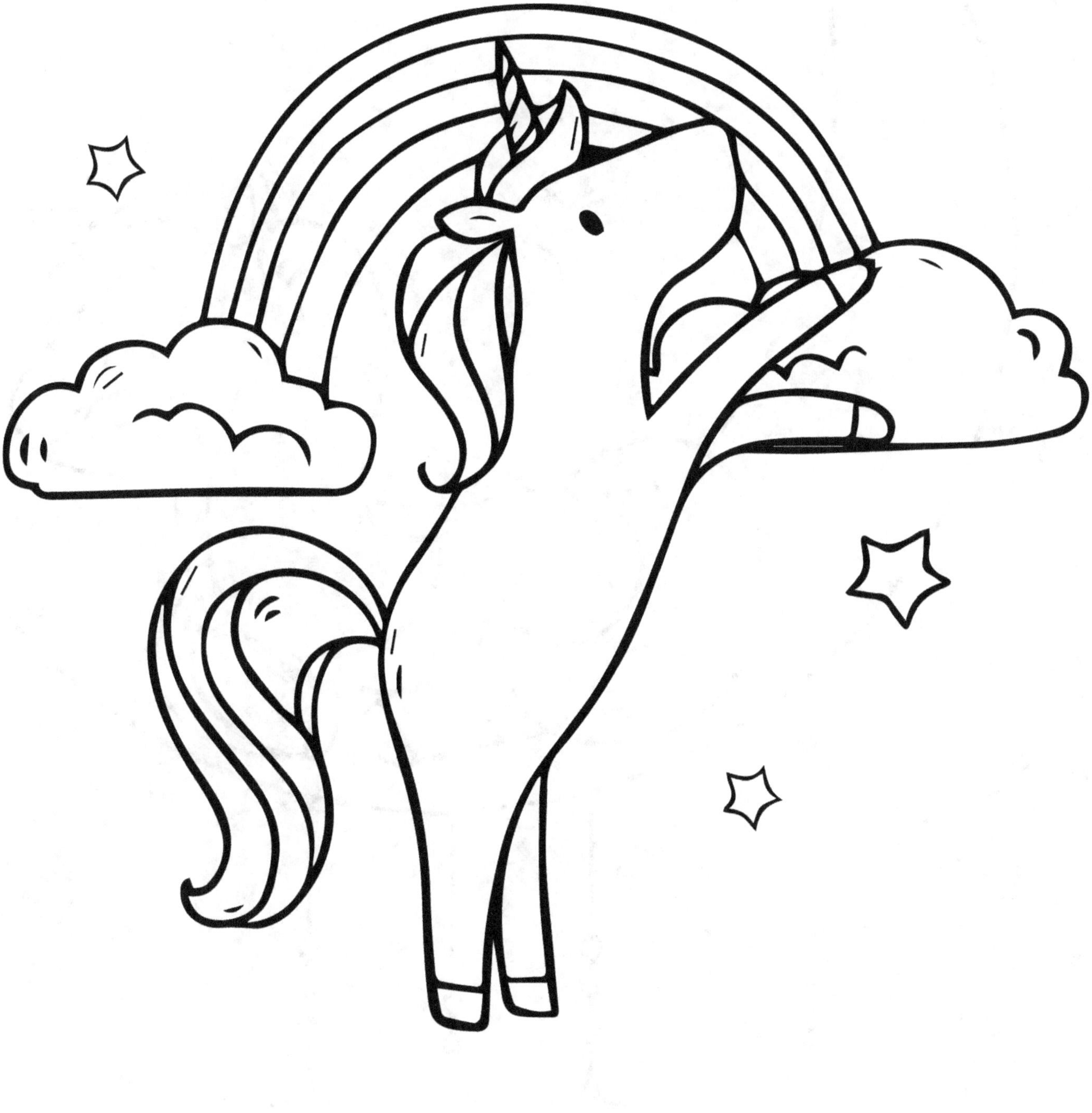

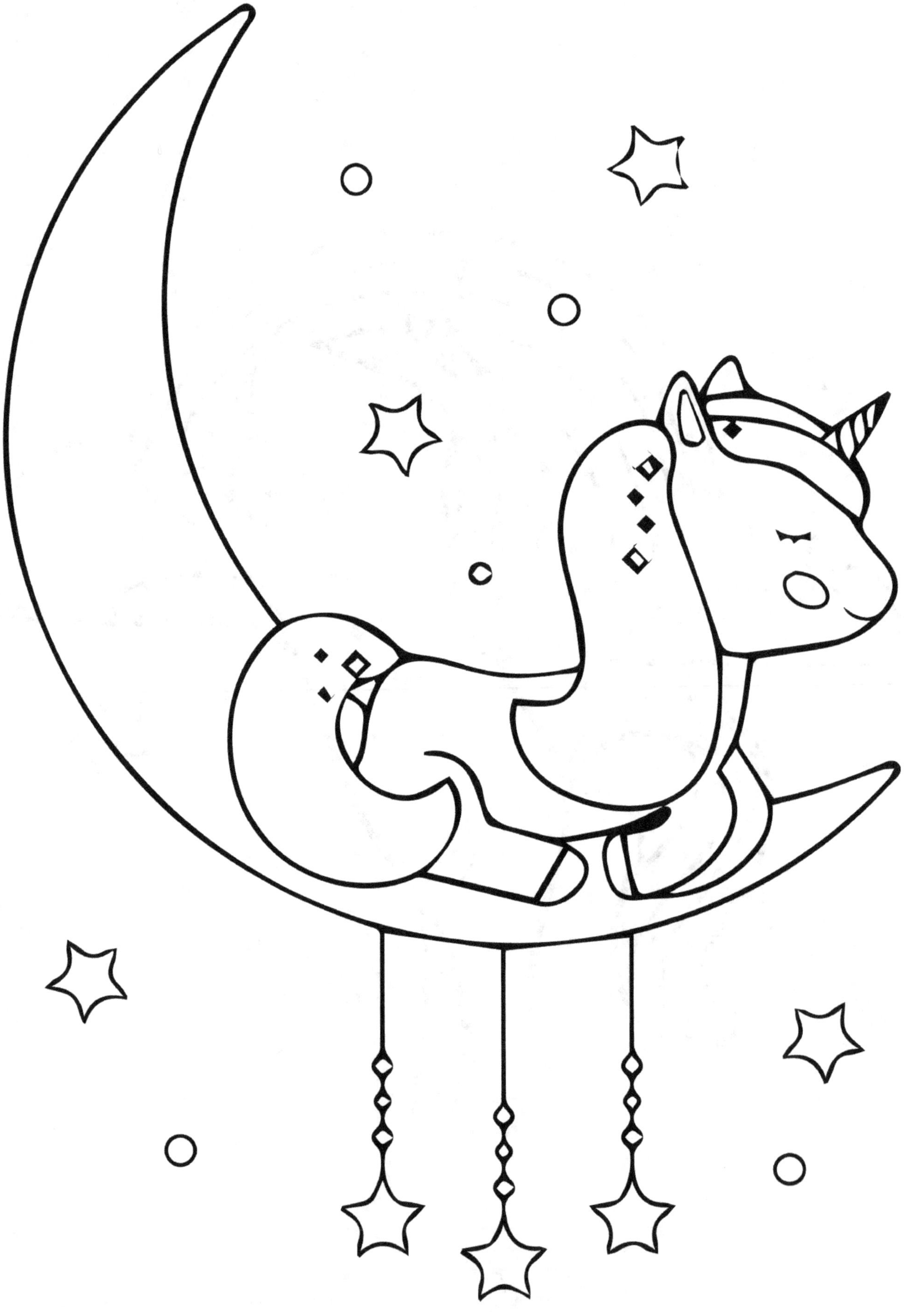

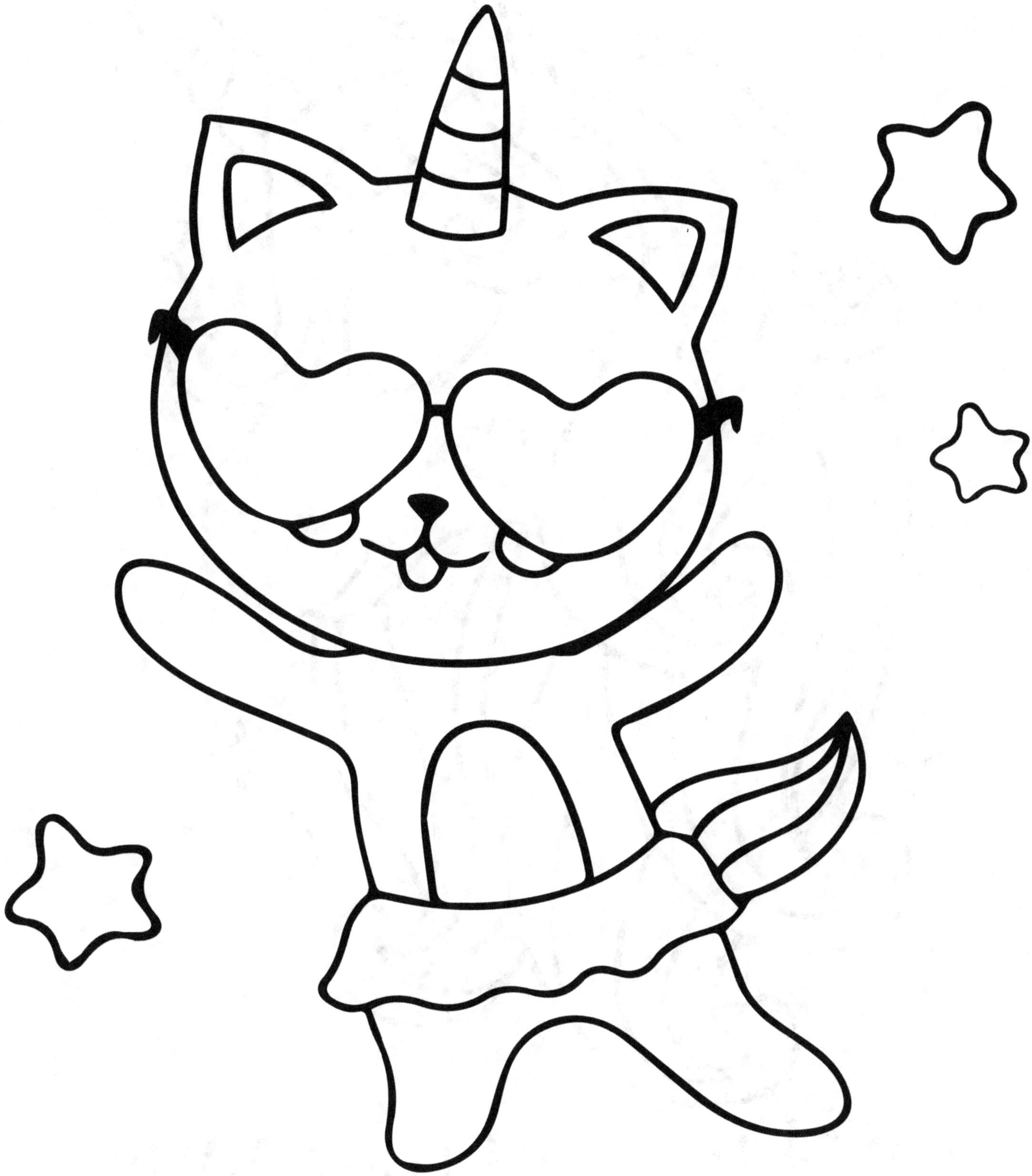

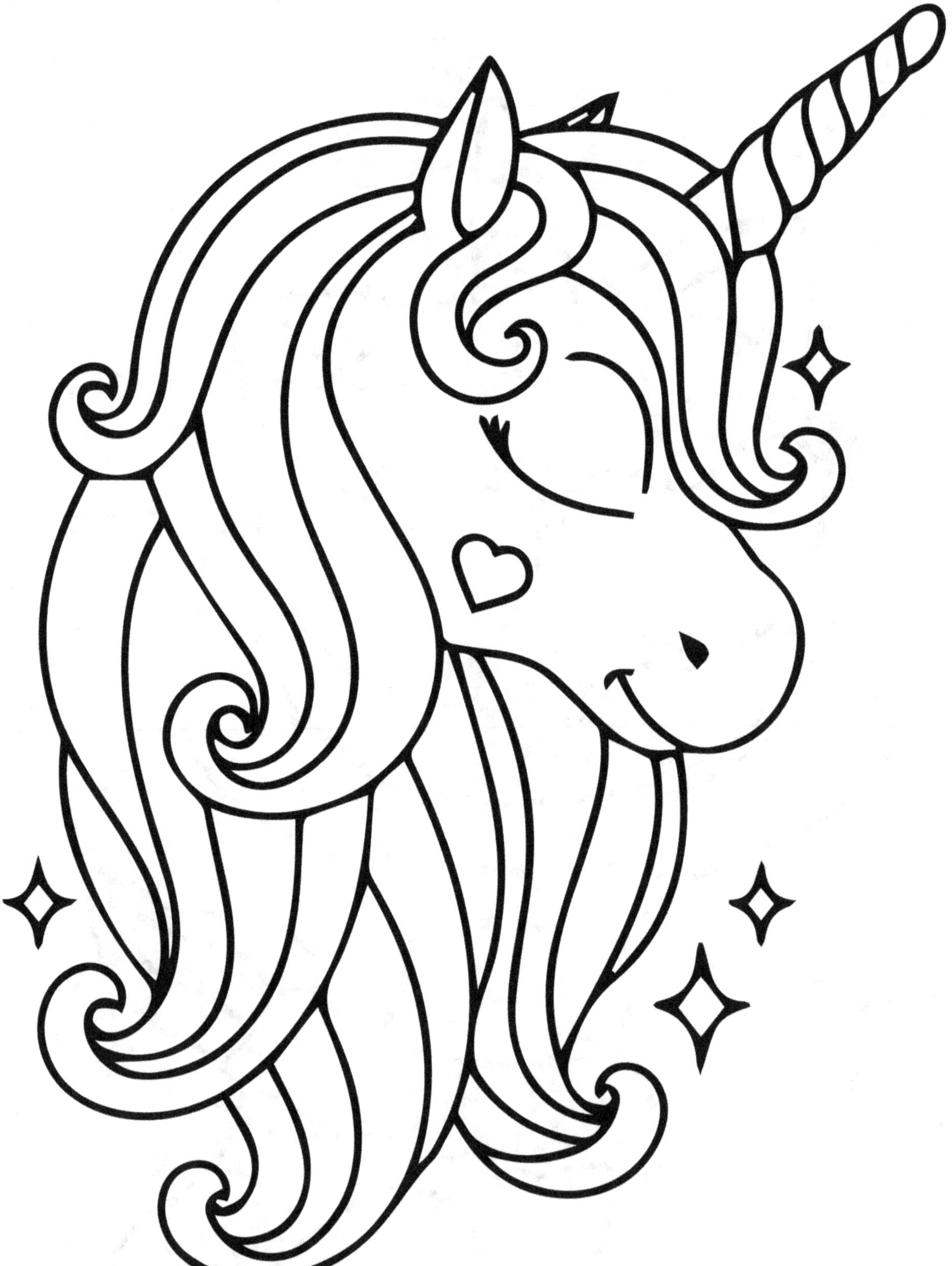

I BELIEVE IN UNICORNS

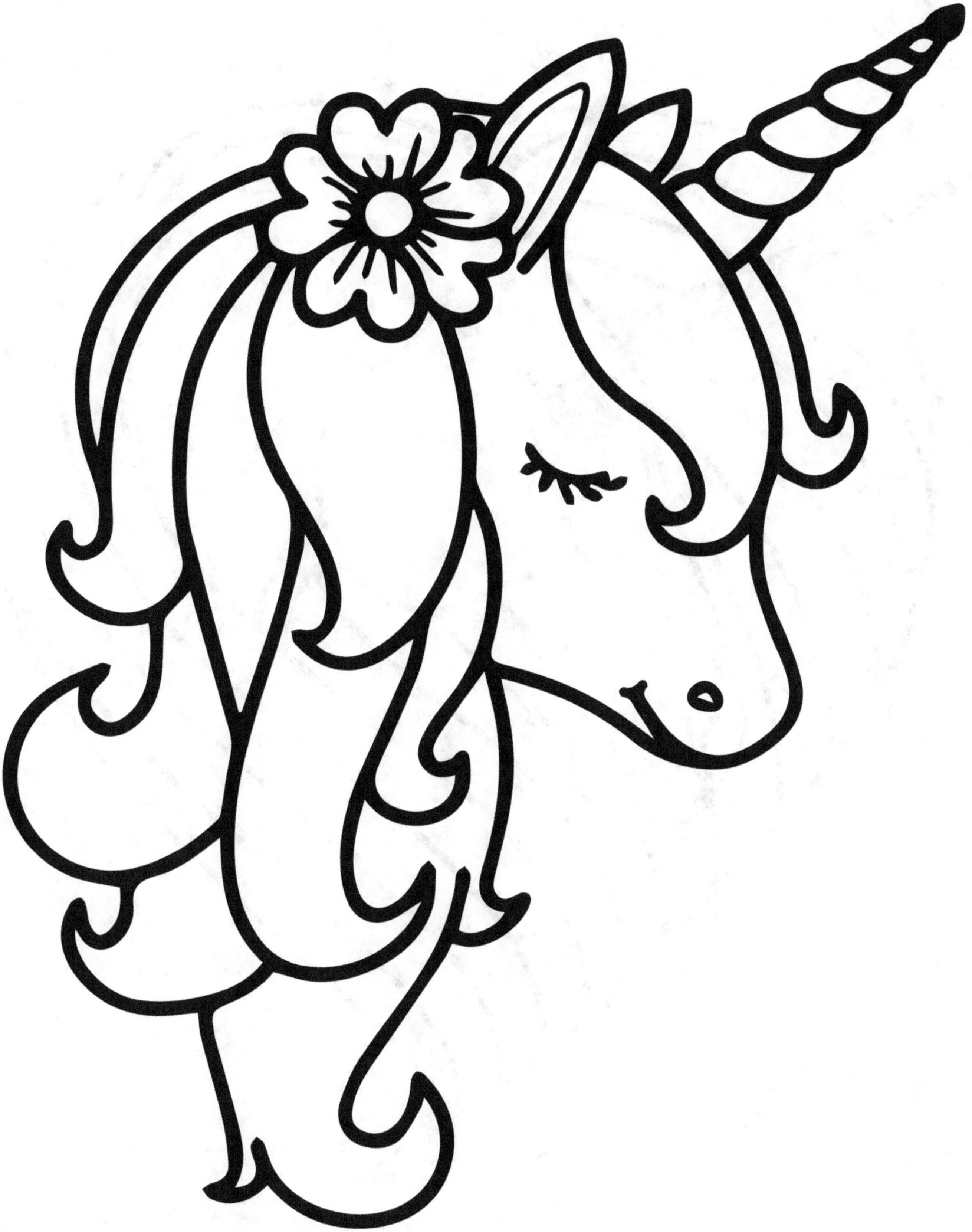

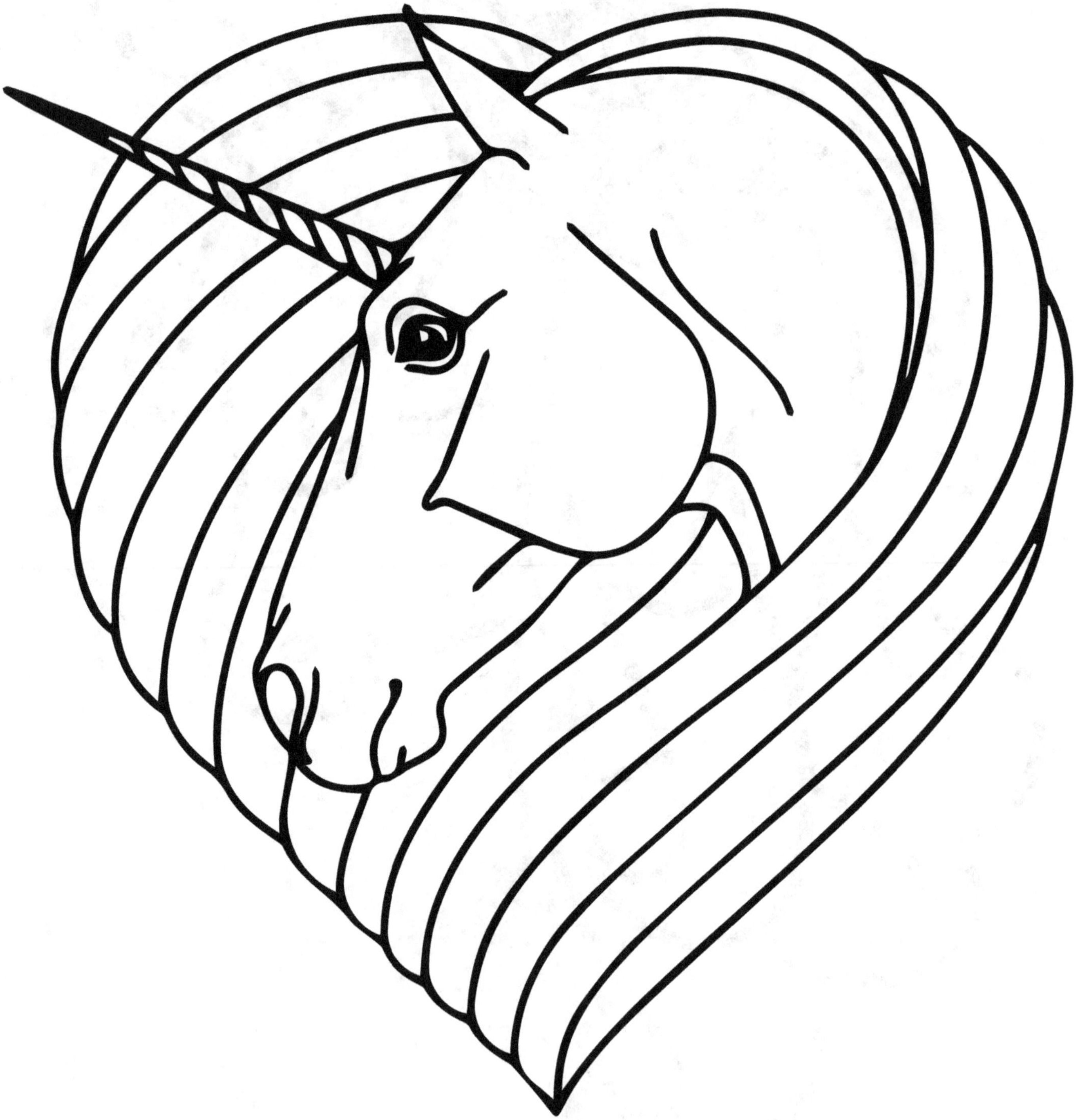

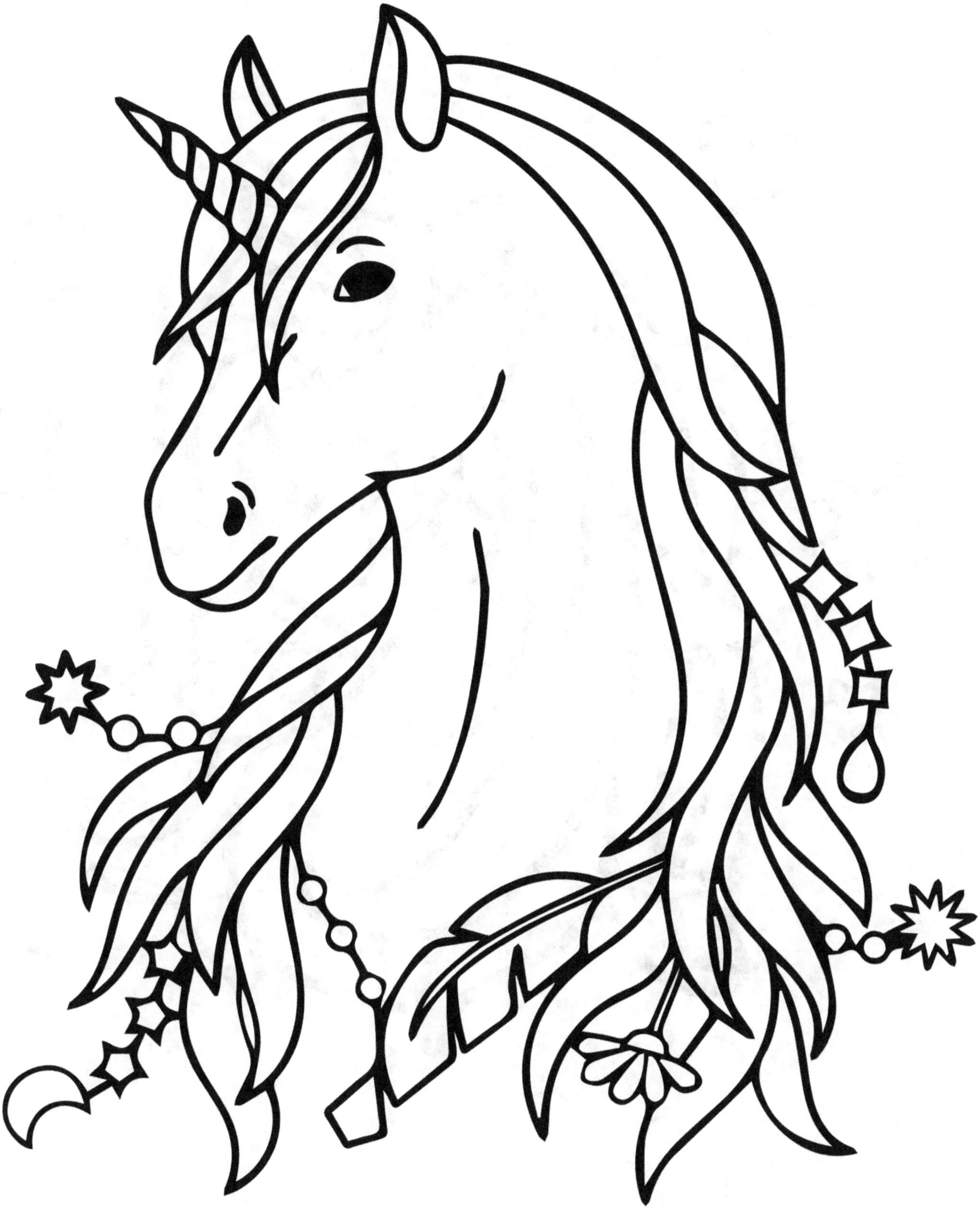

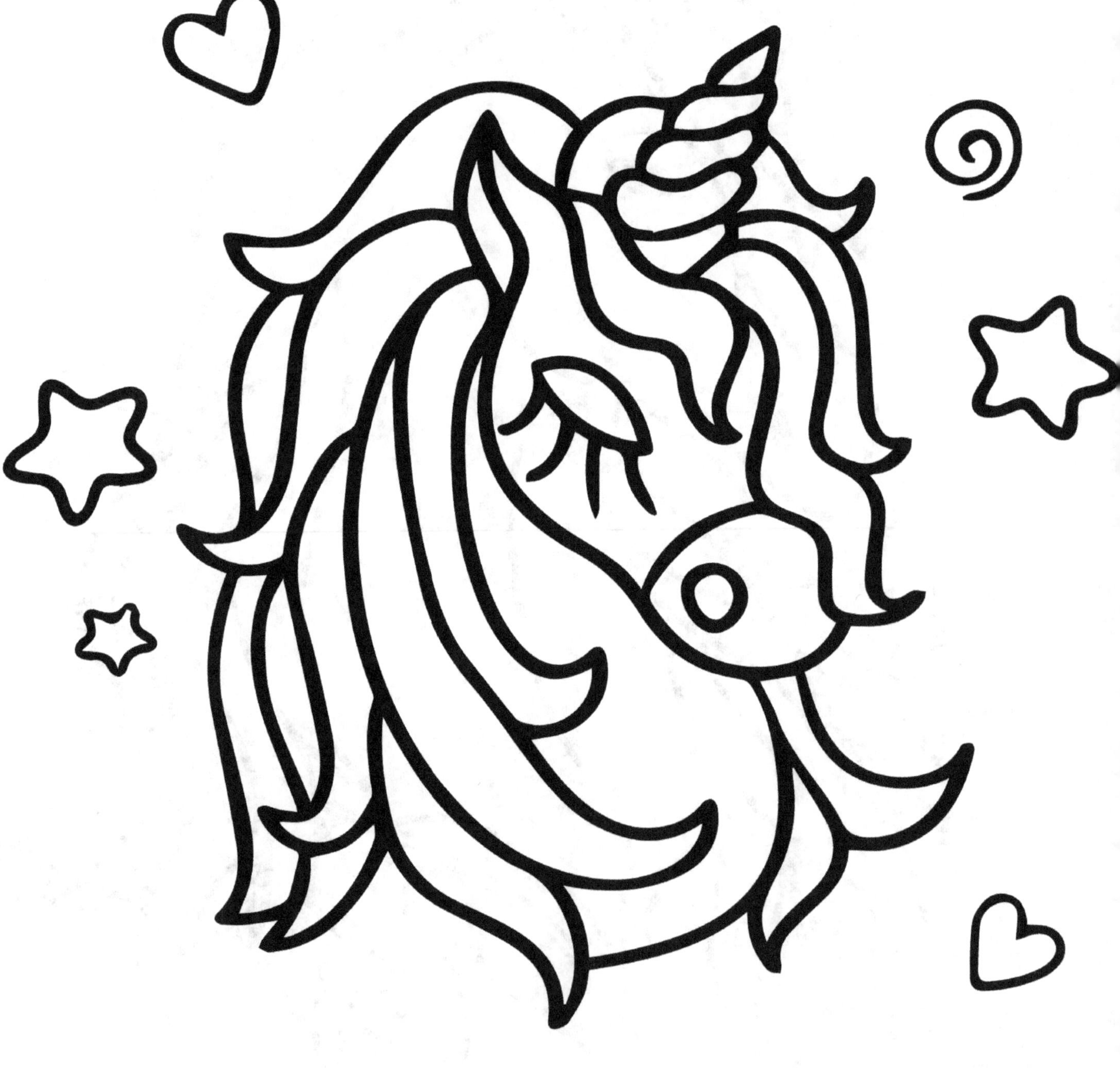

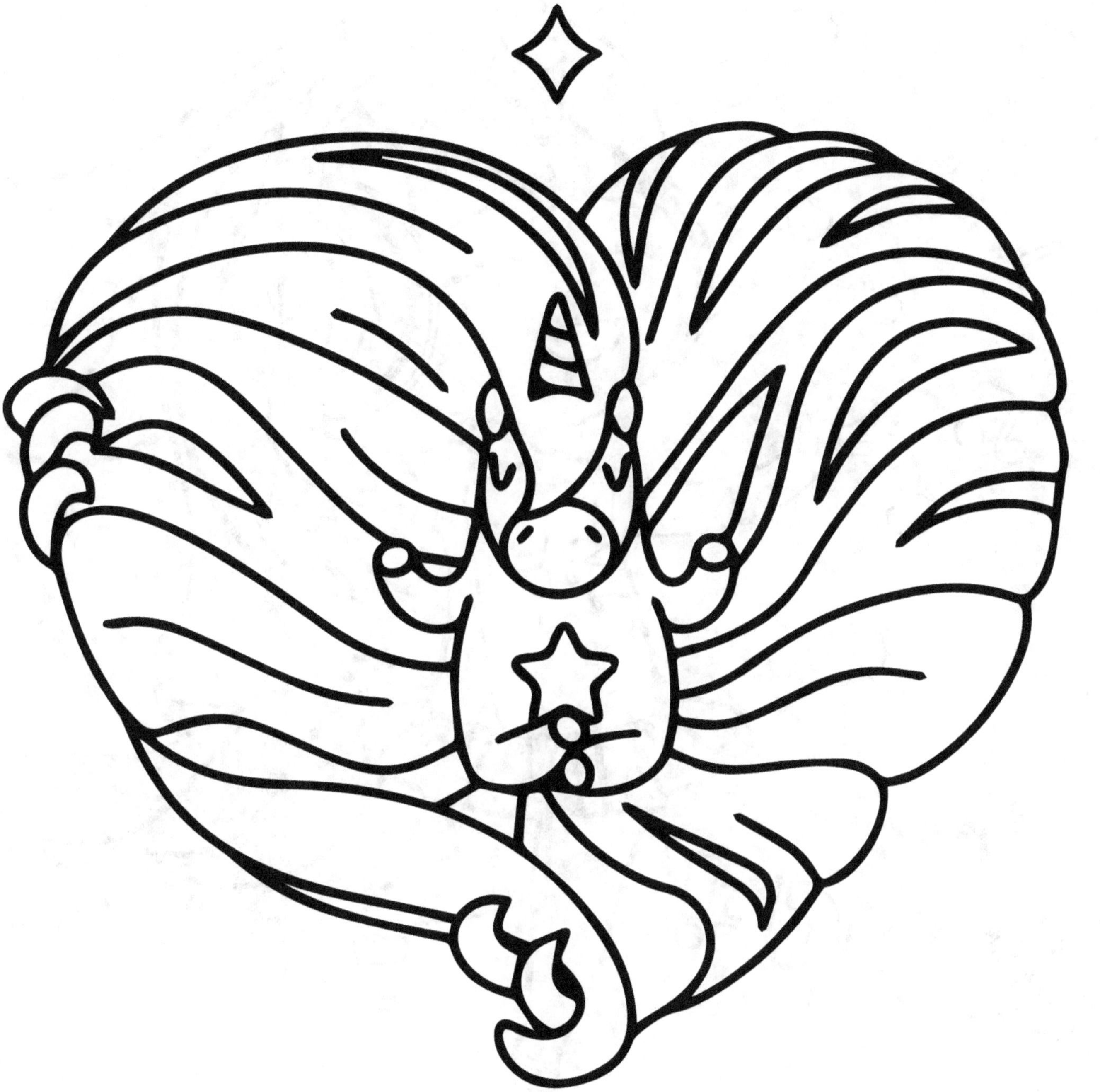

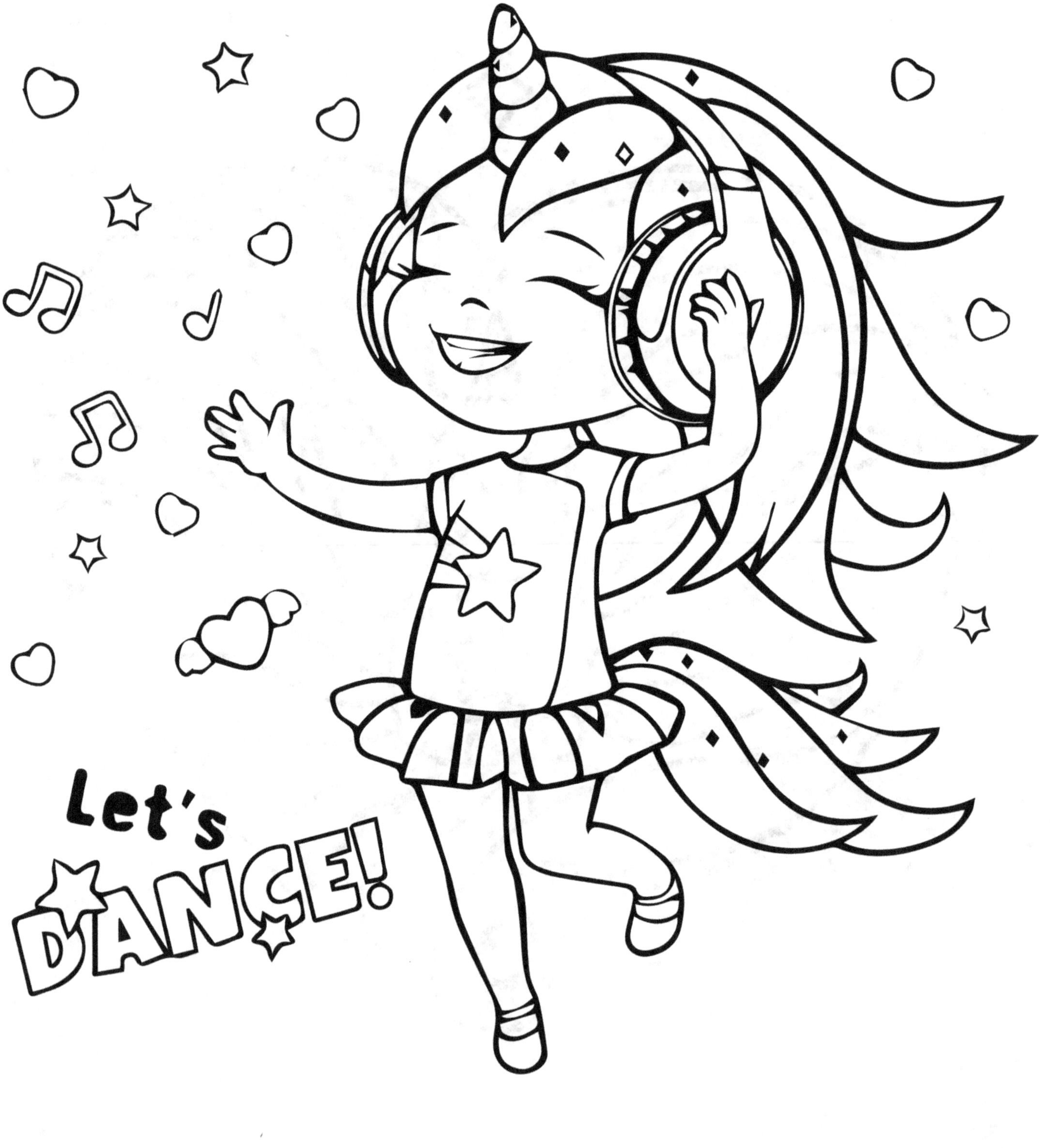
Let's
DANCE!

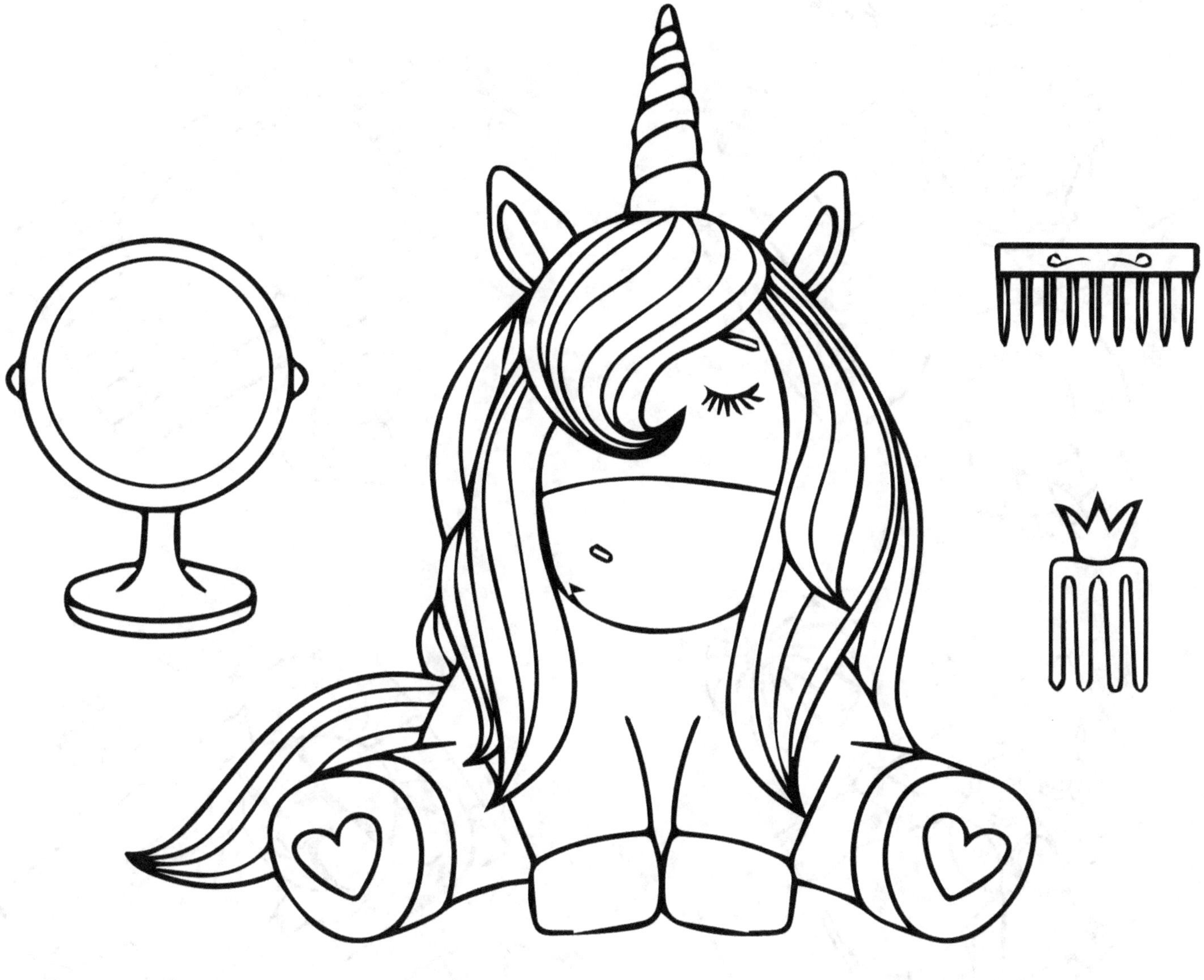

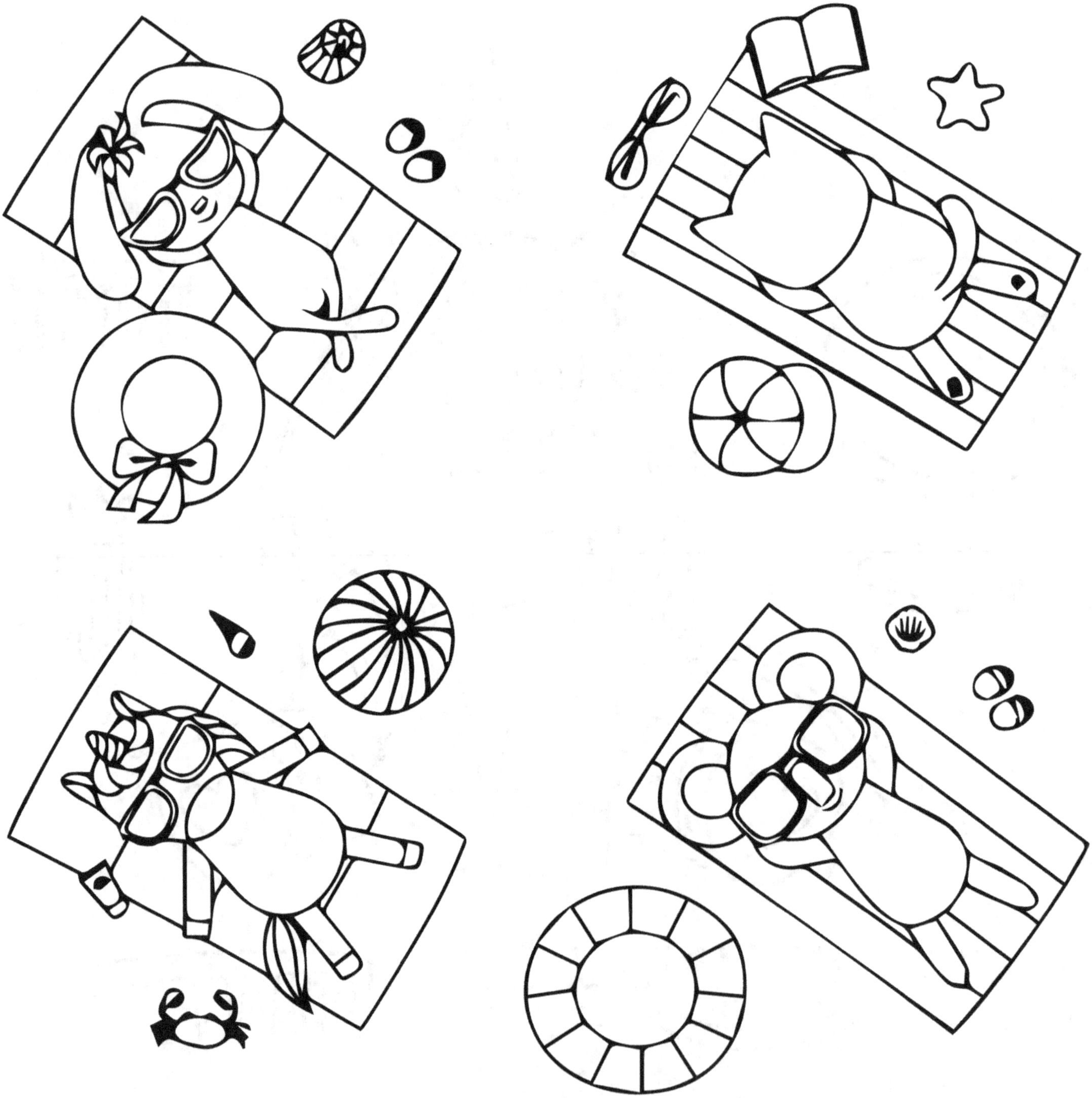

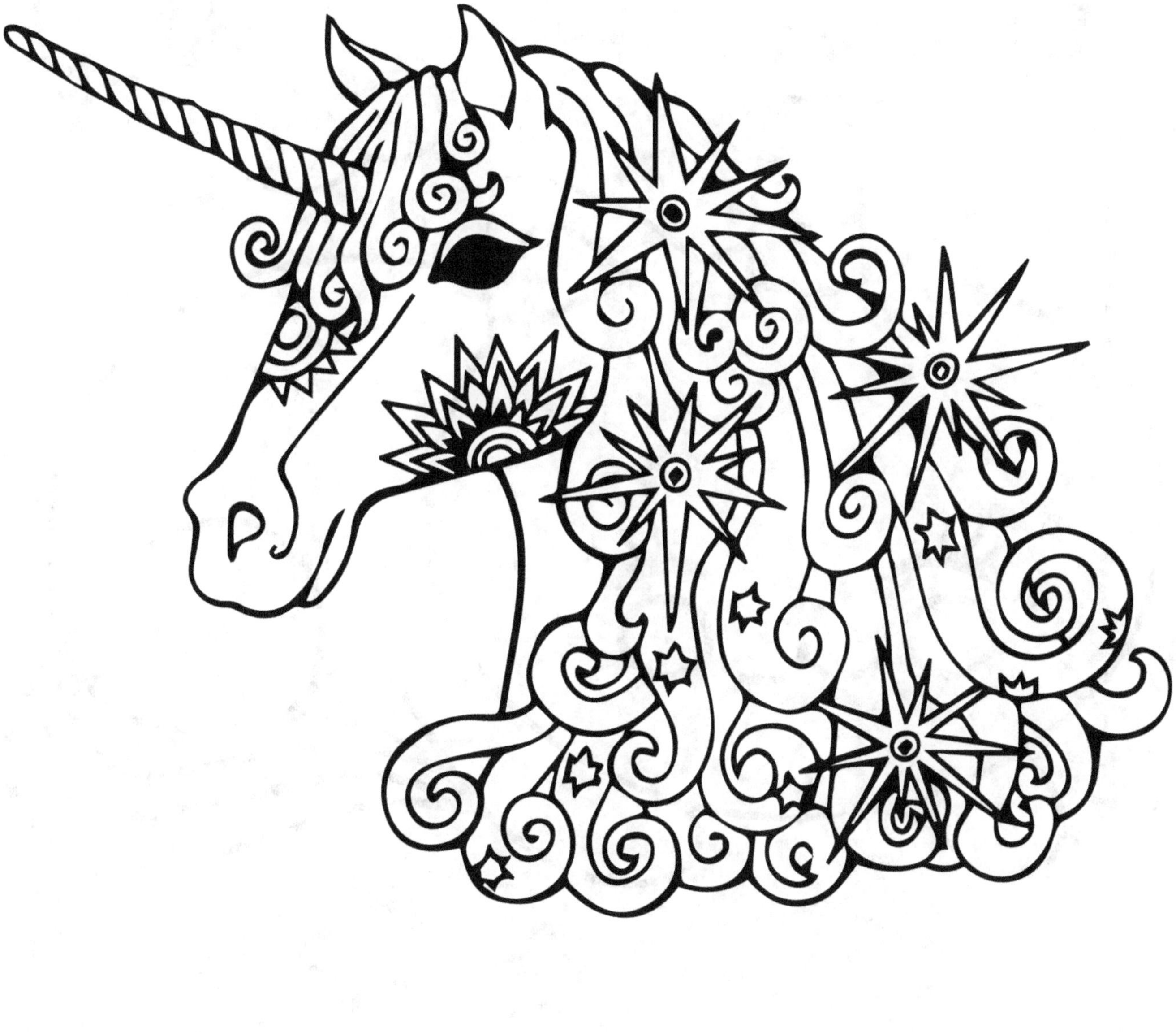

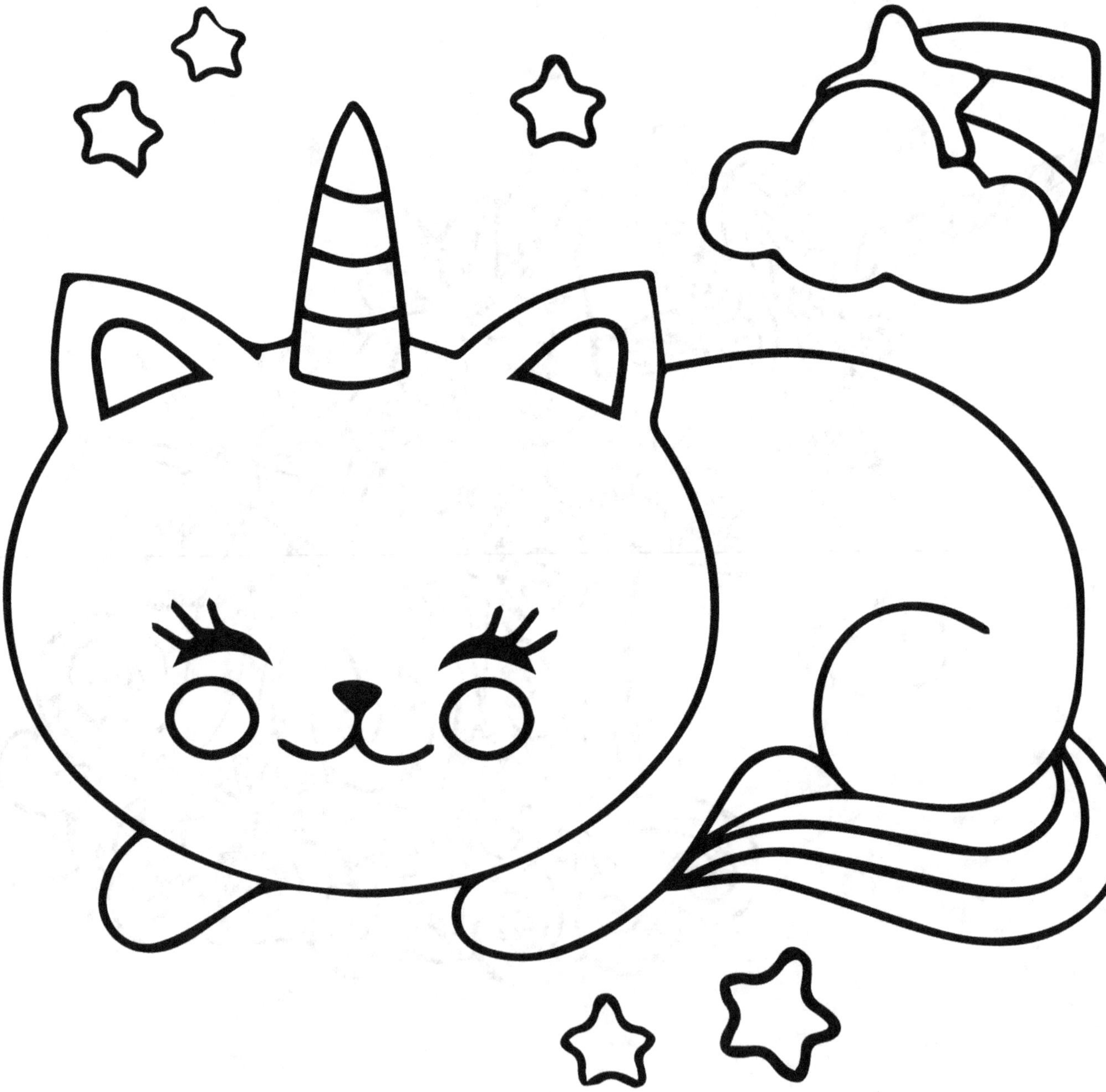

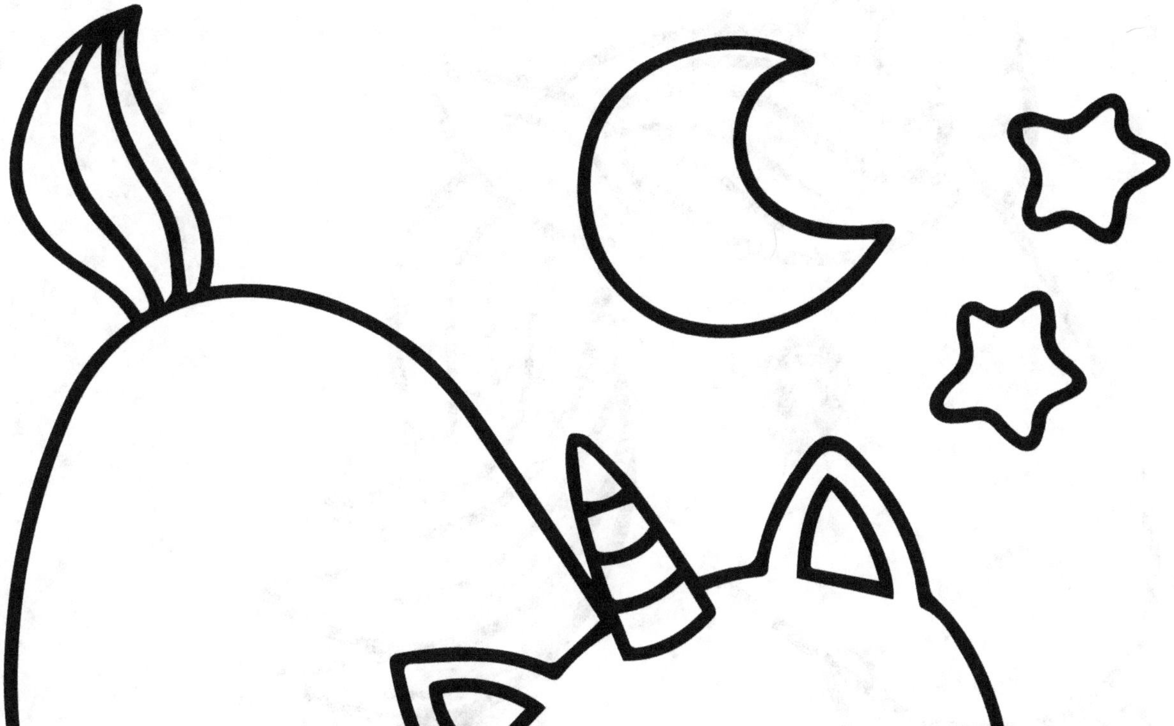

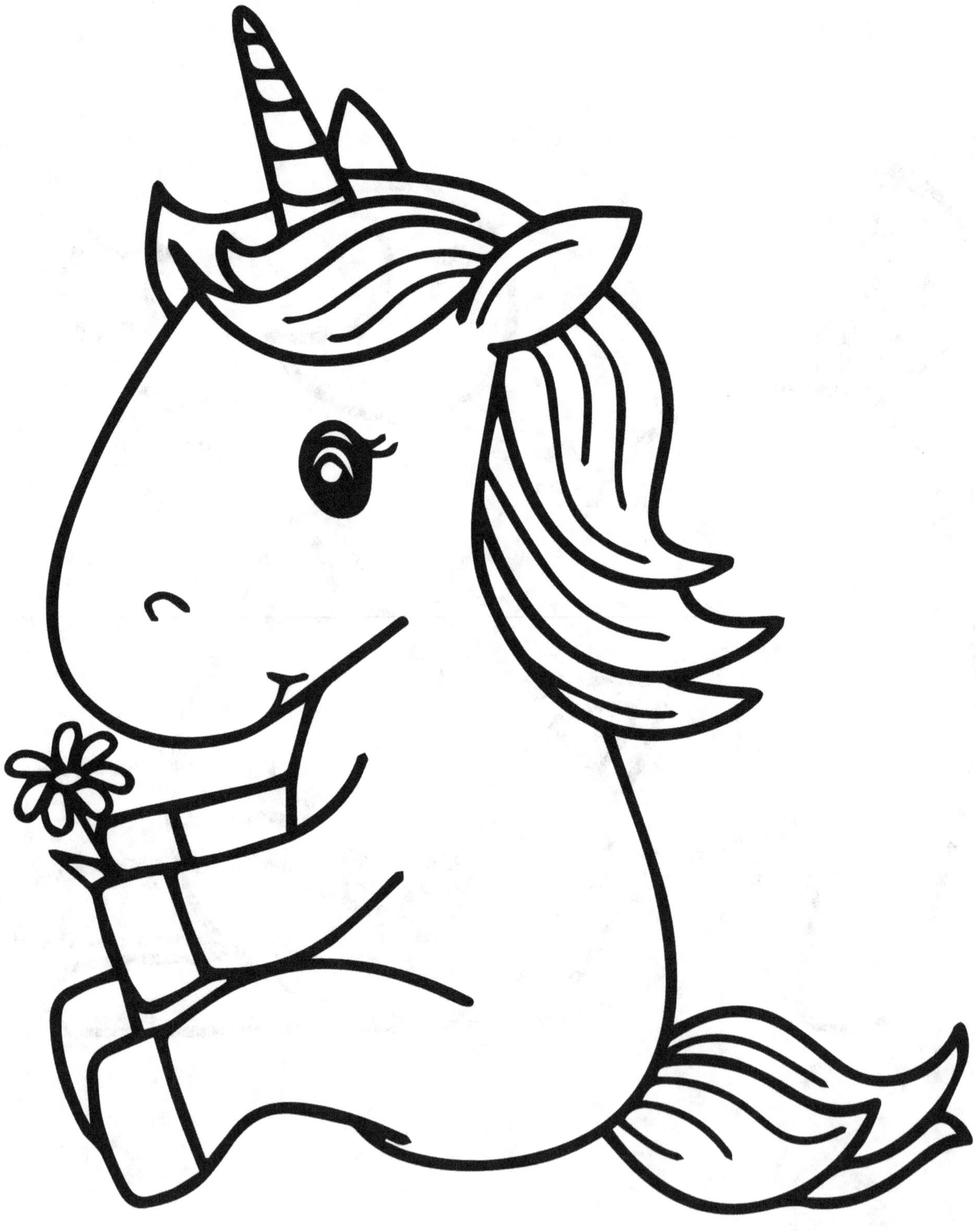

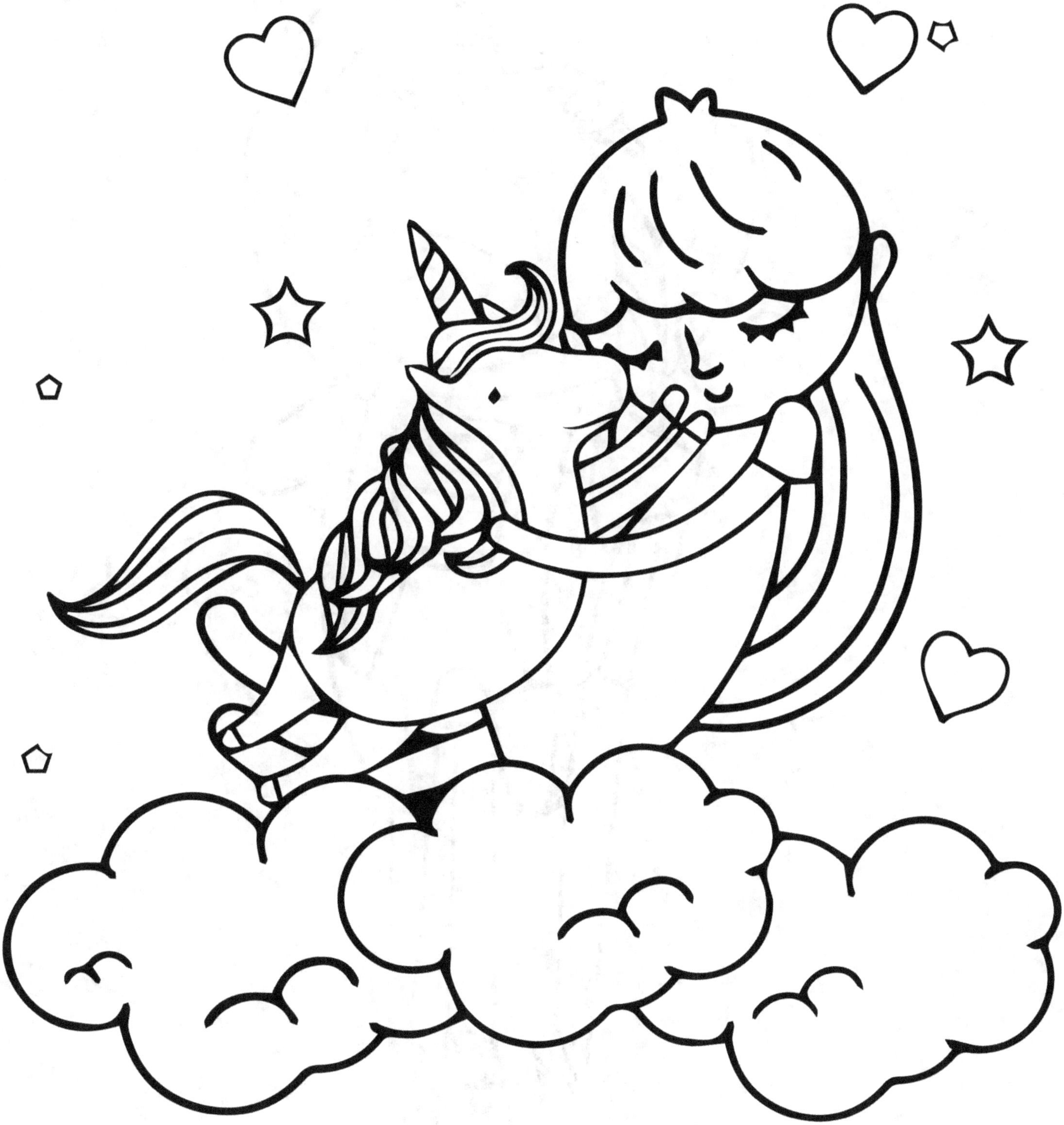

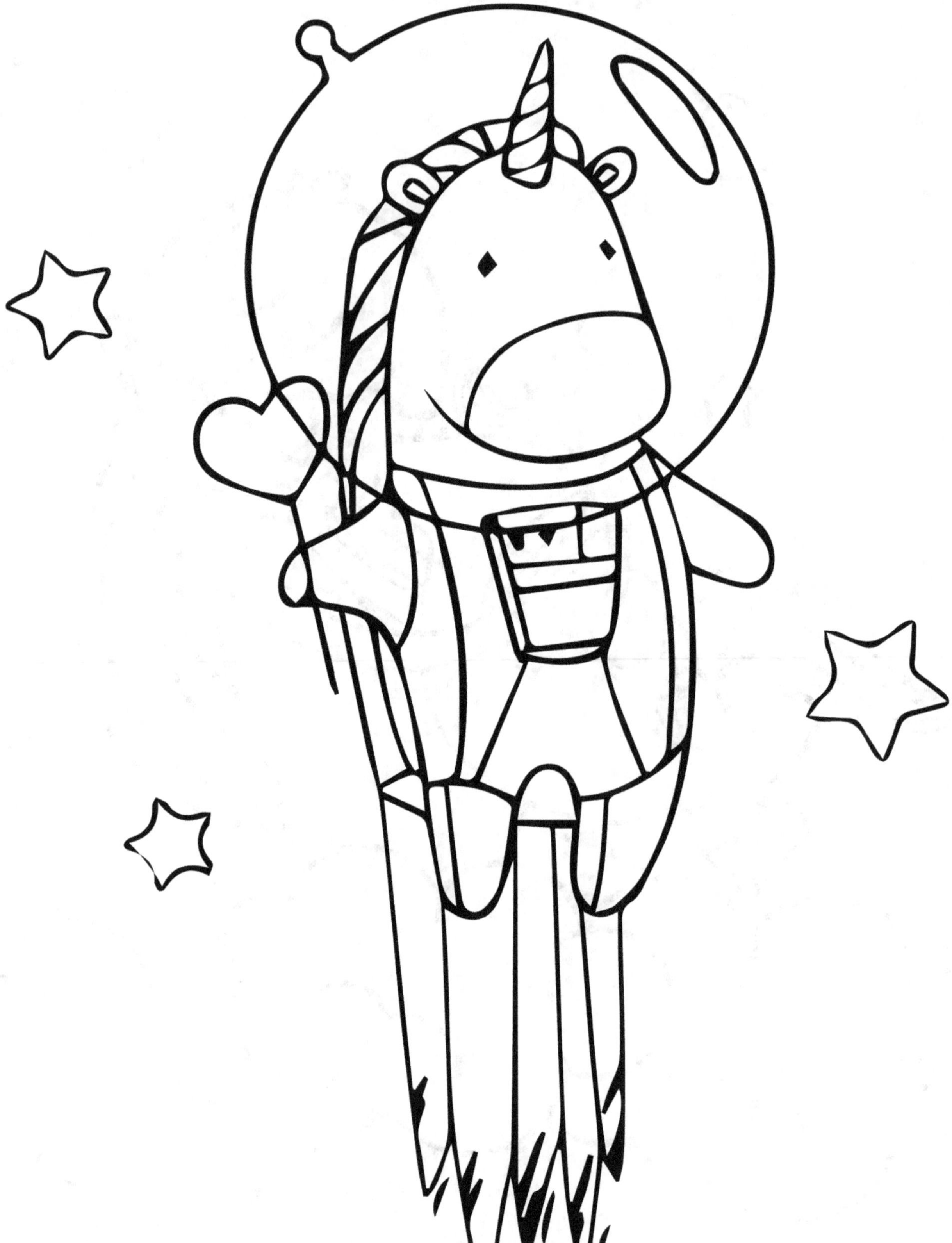

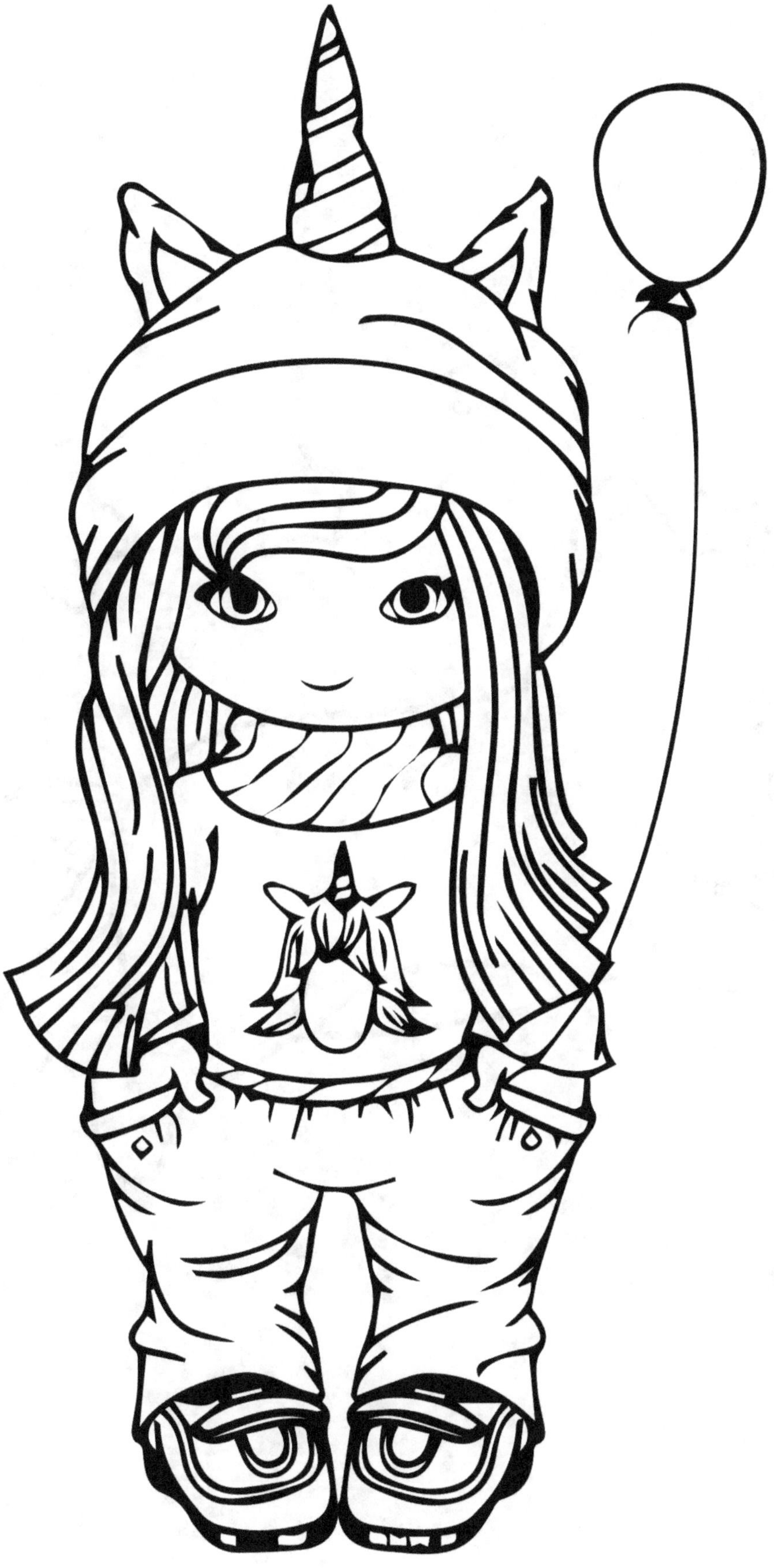

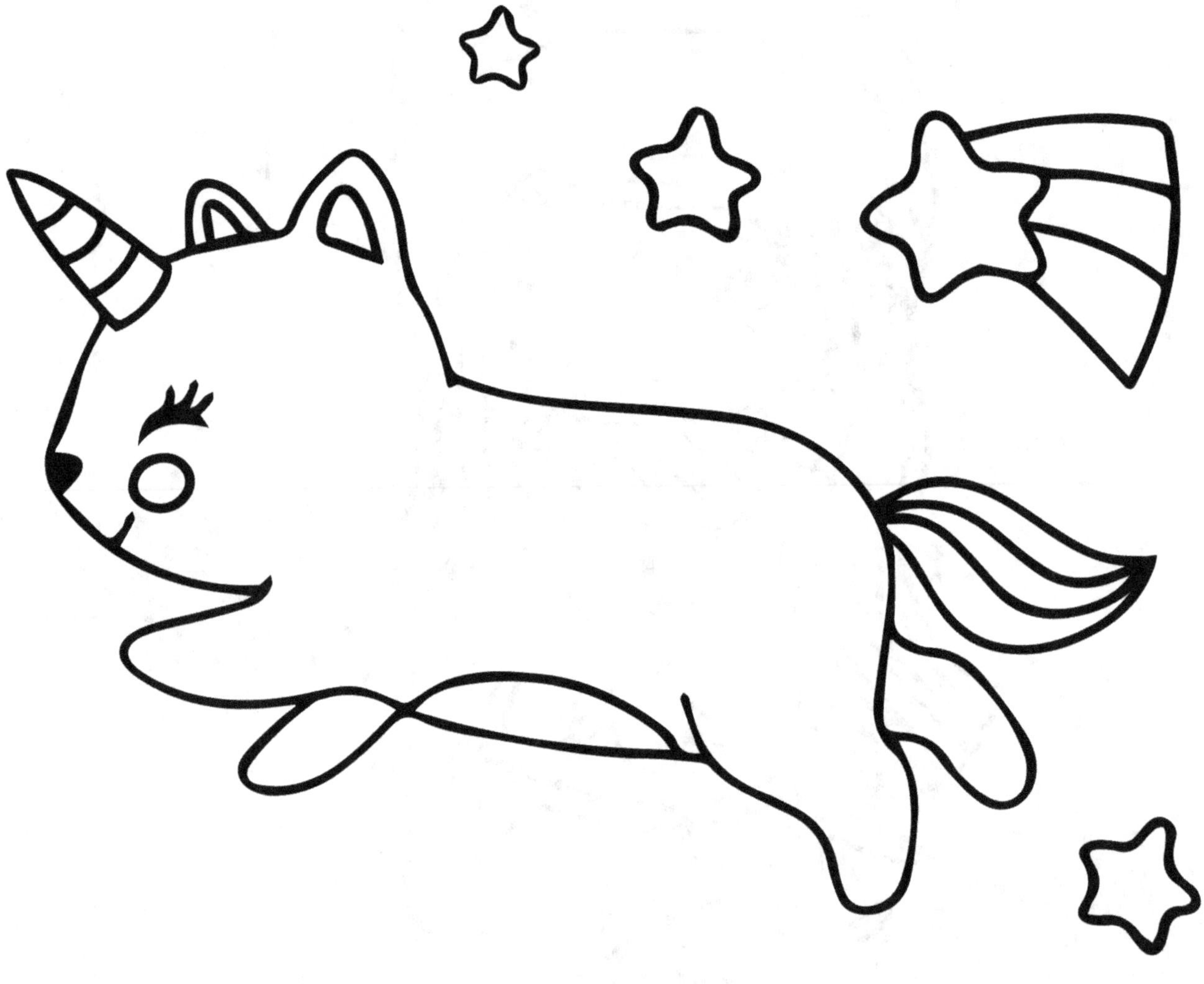

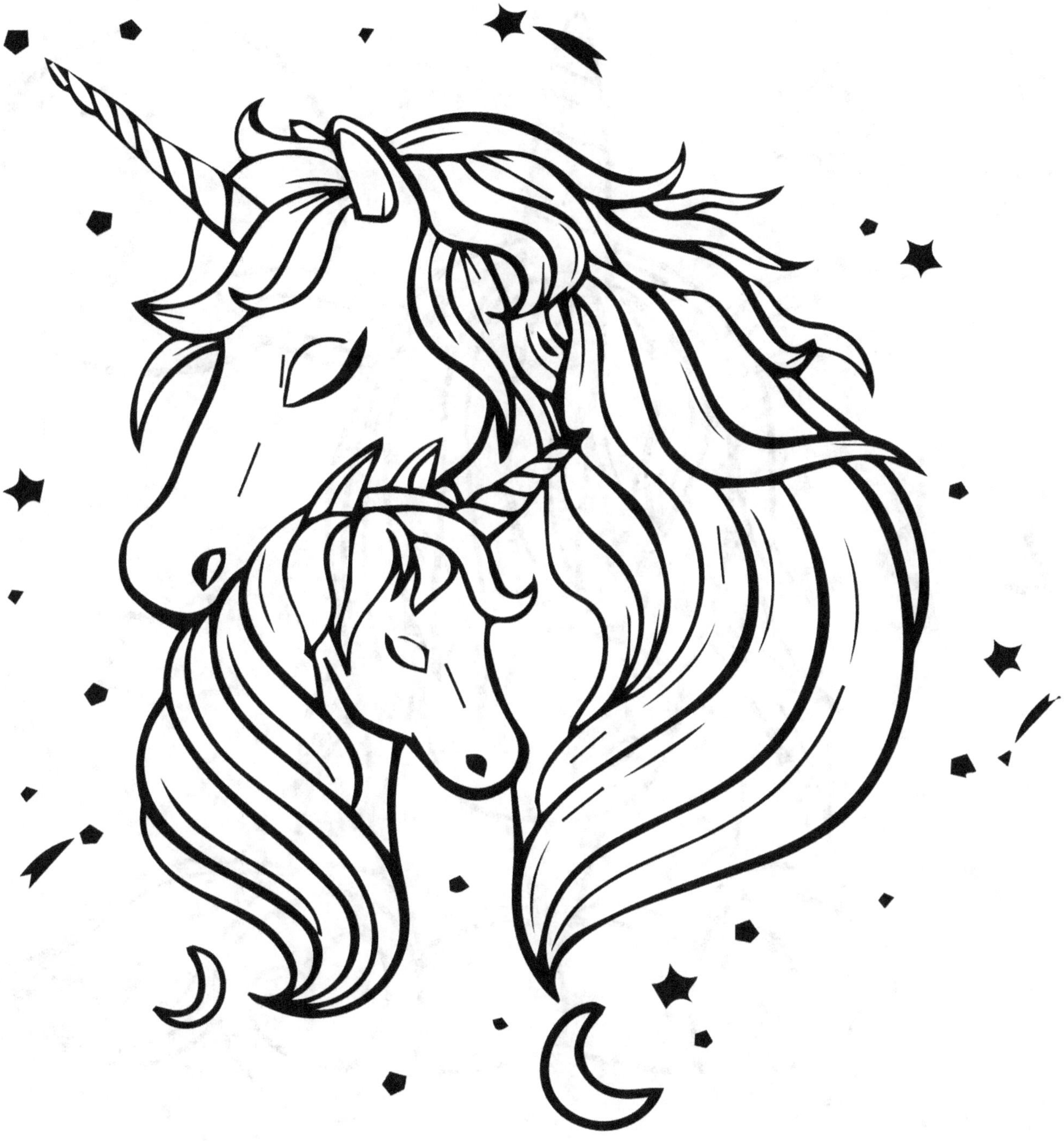

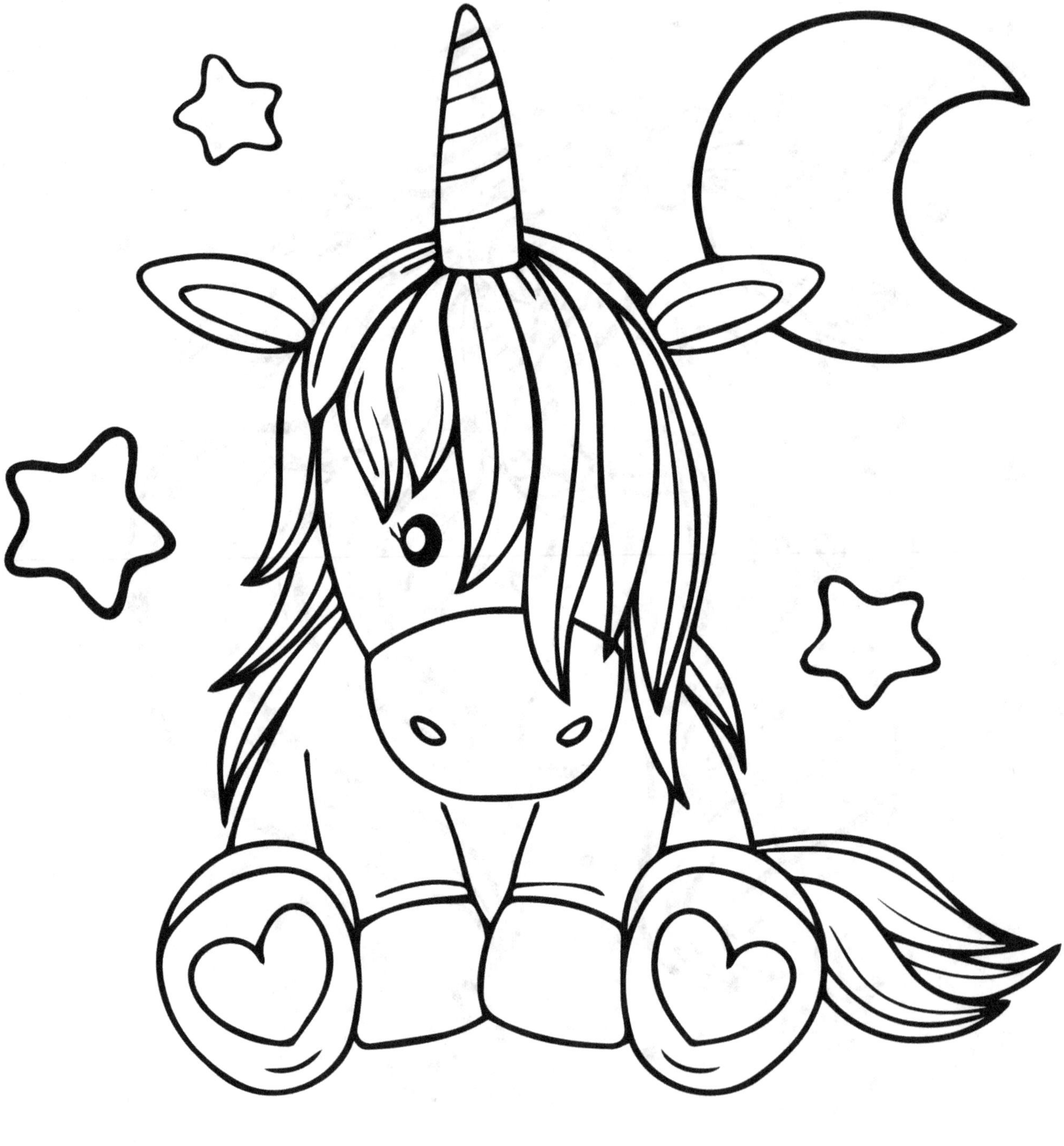

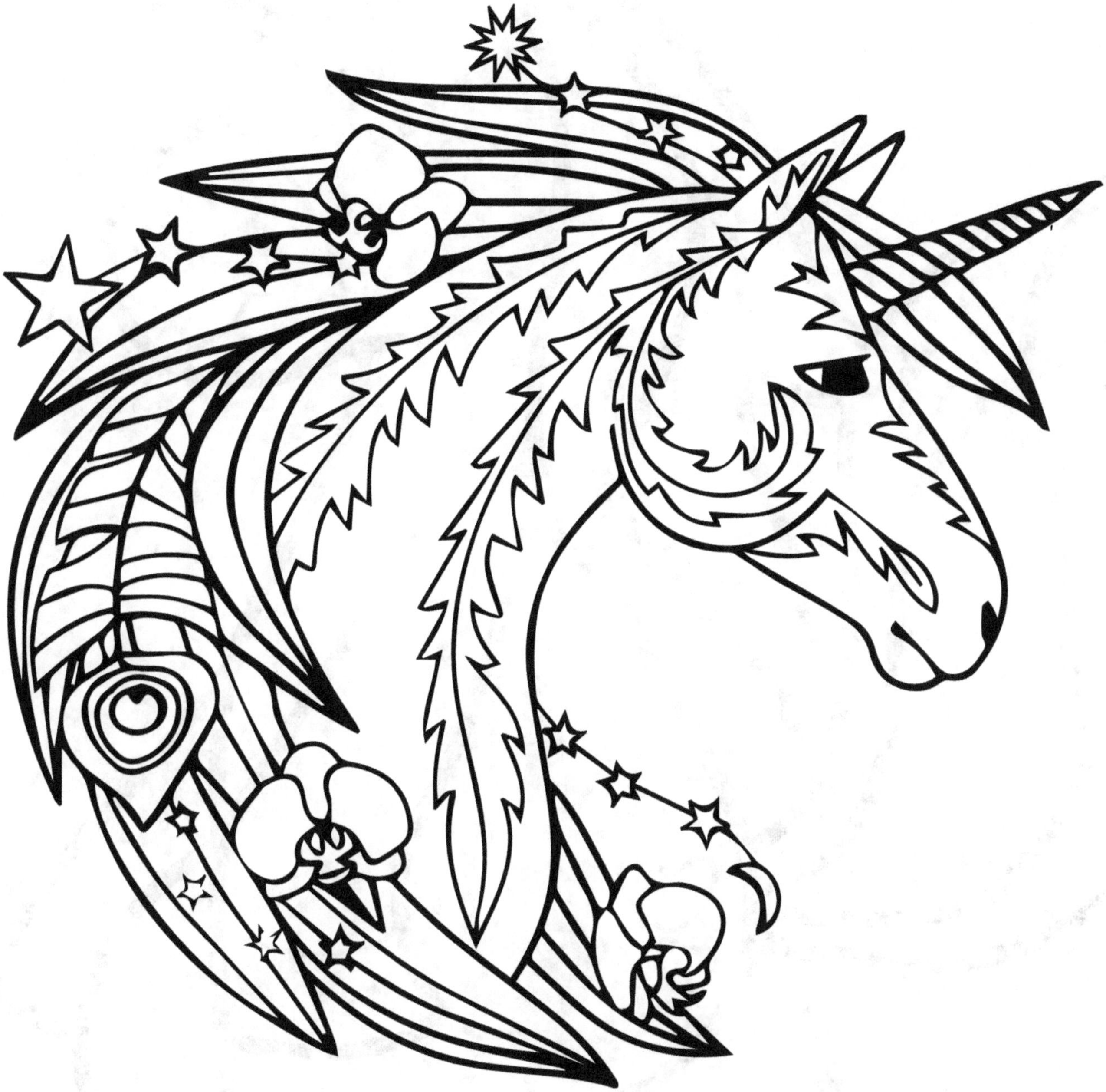

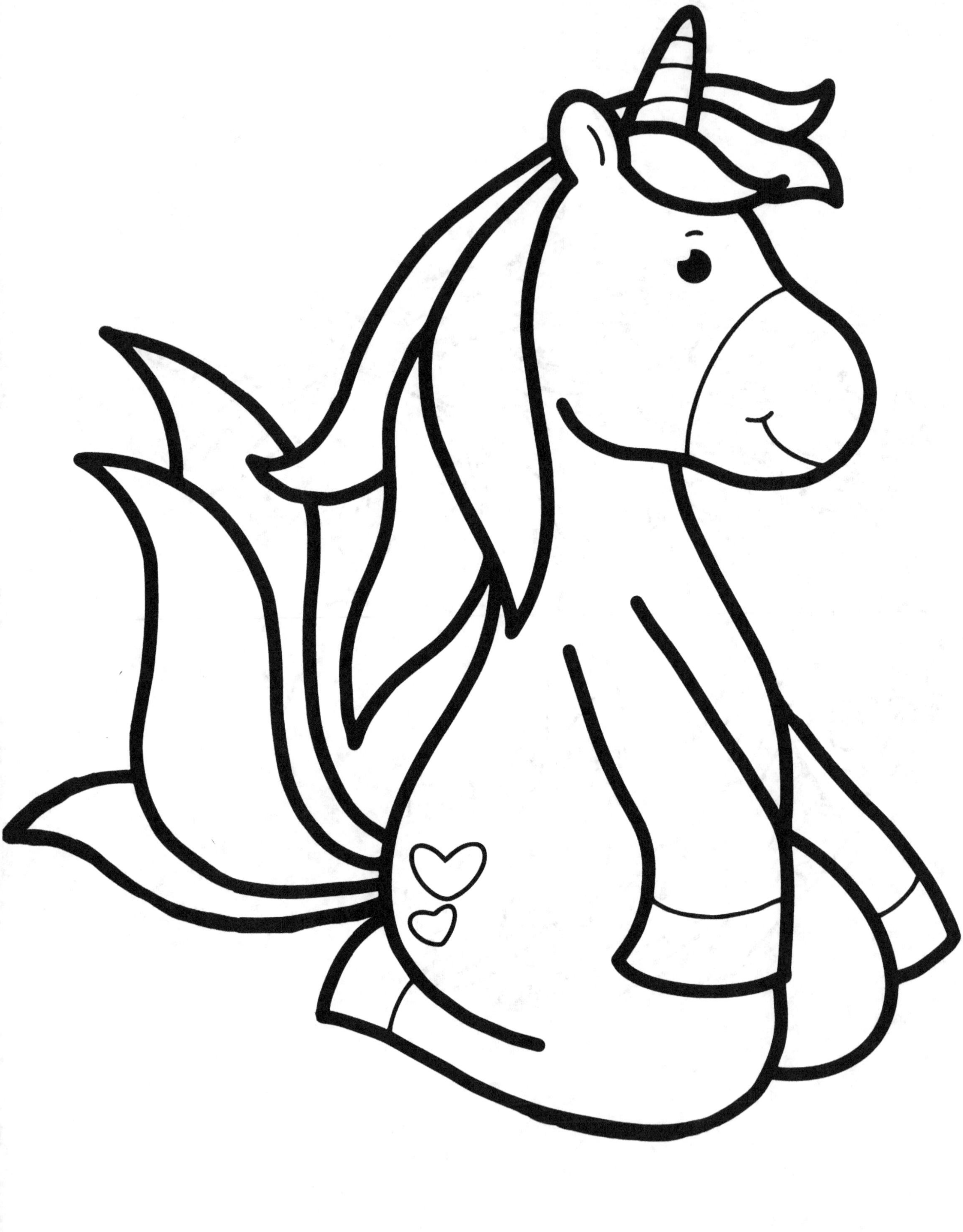

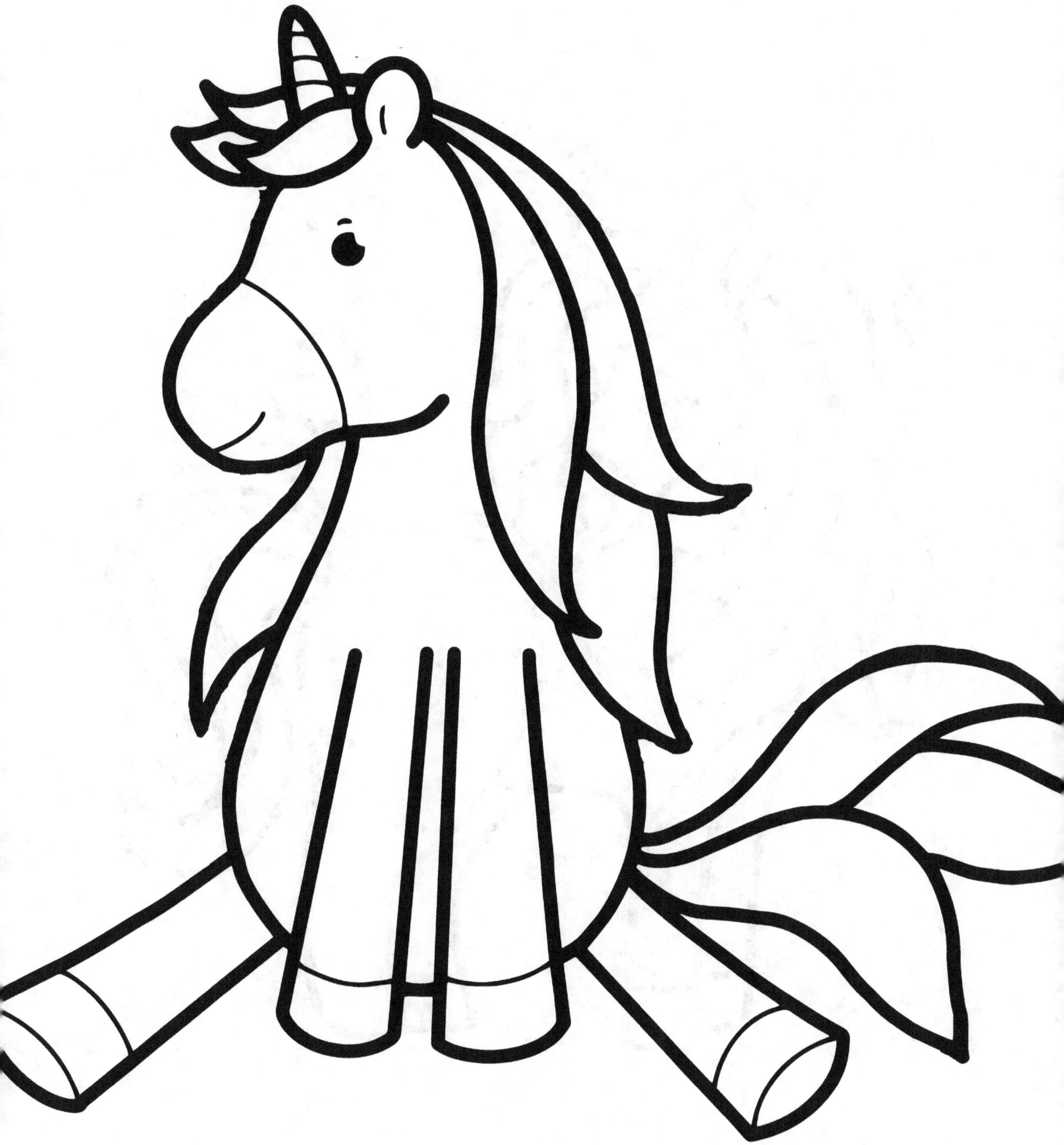

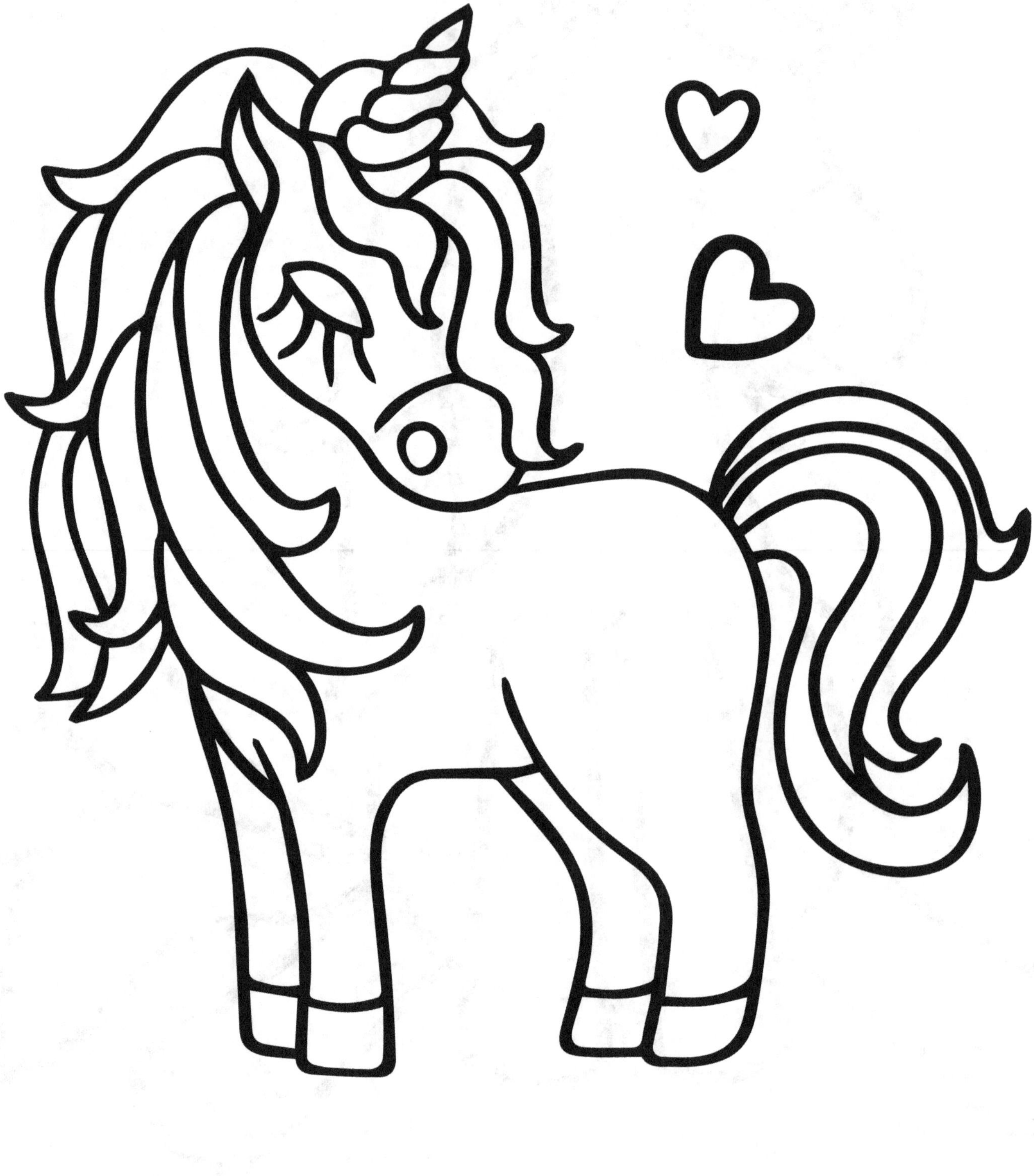

www.ingramcontent.com/pod-product-compliance
Lightning Source LLC
Chambersburg PA
CBHW081528220526
45467CB00010B/3094
9798698818816